ANASAZI

Ancient People of the Rock

HARMONY BOOKS
A DIVISION OF
CROWN PUBLISHERS, INC.
NEW YORK

ANASAZI

Ancient People of the Rock

FOREWORD BY FRANK WATERS   PHOTOGRAPHS BY DAVID MUENCH   TEXT BY DONALD G. PIKE

Pages 2–3: White House ruin, Canyon de Chelly National Monument.

Pages 4–5: Farview House, Mesa Verde National Park.

Pages 6–7: Long House ruin on Wetherill Mesa, Mesa Verde.

Special Consultant: Dr. Robert H. Lister
                      Director, Chaco Canyon Archaeological Center
                      University of New Mexico

Published by Harmony Books, a division of Crown Publishers, Inc.,
201 East 50th Street, New York, New York 10022

HARMONY and colophon are trademarks of Crown Publishers, Inc.
Manufactured in Hong Kong

Library of Congress Cataloging-in-Publication Data
Muench, David.
   Anasazi: ancient people of the rock.
   Reprint. Originally published: Palo Alto, Calif.:
American West Pub. Co., © 1974.
   Includes index.
   1. Pueblo Indians—Antiquities.   2. Indians of North
America—Southwest, New—Antiquities.   3. Southwest,
New—Antiquities.   I. Pike, Donald G.   II. Title.
E99.P9M9   1986   979'.01   85-27272

ISBN 0-517-52690-5
10 9 8 7 6 5 4

First Harmony Edition, 1986

Contents

Foreword
by Frank Waters

This magnificent book comes to us from the publishers of *Living Water*, *This Living Earth*, *The Great Southwest*, and other notable volumes. Their very titles indicate an important psychological change in American outlook now under way. We are no longer wholly dedicated to the belief that the earth is a vast jackpot of inanimate natural resources to be exploited for our material gain. This is particularly true here in the Southwest, where we are greatly disturbed by the ravages of the technological juggernaut and are making efforts to restrain further exploitation of the last open land, pure air, and clean water in this heartbreakingly beautiful heartland of America. We are slowly inclining to the Indian belief that nature is not inanimate, but imbued with one common life-force: the living water and living earth, mountains, trees, plants, animals, and man. All are born of Mother Earth, all are bound together in unbroken continuity, in an indivisible unity of both biological and spiritual ecology.

How can we account for this change? Simply that from the deep unconscious, the earth itself—the substratum of man's essential being—is reemerging in archetypes of wholeness and unity. And this is reflected in our changing pictorial art style.

For many years our art, which like all art is dictated by unconscious drives, has not been concerned with representation of dynamic natural forms. It has generally reflected, instead, an unconscious perception of the fragmentation of all ordered forms under the press of our ethic of materialism. But now our pictorial art especially is changing back from abstract to representational forms. The fecund earth with which we had lost contact is appearing again with all its human derivatives and meanings.

If the European cave drawings of prehistoric bison in the Ice Age and the pictographs and petroglyphs crudely pecked and painted by the ancient Indians of the American Southwest are indeed such symbols, so too must be many examples of modern photography when they attain the dimensions of high art. It is a truism that they are achieved, not by the mechanical perfection of the camera, but by the eye which directs it, the mind which selects its focus, and behind these, the unconscious which perceives the essence of the subject. David Muench, like his father Josef, is a great photographer. So we need not question why, during this technological age, his photographic art has been devoted to interpretive depictions of the great Southwest, through which he has wandered for many years.

These considerations may help to explain why his nine pictorial portfolios in this book are imbued with such emotional values. They are not merely tourist "Views of the Scenic Southwest"; they reflect the order, wholeness, and unity inherent in the earth itself. We can experience the numinous quality of their living essence, the religious quality intuited by the Indians of ancient America. For in us, too, the emerging contents of our inner selves are giving us a new vision of old forms.

Not the most pessimistic of us can doubt, upon turning these pages, that the spirit of place is still asserting itself. This is what makes this book so timely, affirming our awakened interest in the great Southwest and its first known dwellers.

I have often wondered how we Anglos came to adopt the use of the Navajo name *Anasazi*, "The Ancient Ones," for these people. Many Pueblo Indians reject this name for their ancestors, and with good reason. It seems that some fifteen hundred years after their people had been living here in permanent homes, a strange tribe of wild barbarians began to trickle in. The Hopis called them Tavasuh, derived from Tusavuhta (*tu*—person, *savuhta* —to pound), because they killed a captured enemy by pounding his head with a rock or stone club. Today they are known to us as Navajos, a proud, enterprising people who comprise the largest and richest Indian tribe in the United States. Why, then, if the early Navajos are not called by the Pueblo name of Tavasuh, should the ancestors of the Pueblo people be known by the Navajo name of Anasazi?

The cultural history of the Anasazi Pueblo from the beginning of the Christian era to the present is carefully traced in the text by Donald G. Pike. It is divided into many periods: Basket Maker, Modified Basket Maker, Developmental Pueblo, Classic Pueblo, and Pueblo. If the ever-flowing evolutionary course of a vanished people often seems too tidily boxed by this archaeological and anthropological chronology, the author explains the modern techniques of classifying and dating their potsherds and artifacts. The development of exquisite pottery from the first basketware— from which derived the name Basket Makers —is recounted. Also, the structural development of their unique dwellings from crude pithouses dug in the earth to the spectacular cliff dwellings and great multistoried pueblos erected on the open plain, which in turn resulted in their later classification as Pueblos.

It may not be amiss to footnote here another sidelight study of these majestic structures now under way by America's foremost architectural historian, Vincent Scully. Following his comprehensive exposition of the interaction between the early Greek temples and cities and their landscapes in the Hellenic world, he is delineating the architectural relationship of the prehistoric pueblos in the American Southwest with their dramatic landscape. Muench's photographs on the pages that follow amply illustrate the pueblos' superbly aesthetic integration of line and mass with their backdrop of towering cliff walls and skyline of isolated buttes and mesas rising on the horizon. The Anasazi, primitive as he was and plagued with arthritis and toothache, was not only an artisan but an artist.

Where these Ancient Ones came from poses a moot question both to scholarly archaeologists and anthropologists, and to forthright mythicists like myself. The former adhere to the theory of an influx of people from Asia to America by way of the Bering Strait about 15,000 years ago. Gradually these immigrants spread southward throughout the length of the continent, forming pools of primitive culture. One of them was the Cochise, or Desert

Culture, in our Southwest, from which the Basket Makers, or Anasazi, of the San Juan drainage area possibly derived about the time of Christ. A thousand or more years later, culminating with the great drought in the thirteenth century, the Anasazi Pueblo people abandoned their homelands in the Four Corners area and migrated south and east to establish themselves in the pueblos of the Hopi and Zuñi, and those along the Rio Grande.

Hopi myth, on the contrary, recounts that the Hopis crossed the sea during their emergence to this present Fourth World, arriving somewhere on the western coast of Mexico or Central America. They then gradually worked northward to settle in their present homeland in the Four Corners region. The validity of the myth is attested in many ways: the dramatic reenactment of their migratory journey in numerous ceremonials, the many place names of their identified settlements along the way, and the similarity of their rituals to those of the highly civilized peoples of ancient Mesoamerica.

The vast scope of the present text includes the relationship of the Anasazi culture with the Mogollon and Hohokam cultures to the south, and also the probability of Mexican influences reaching the Southwest, as shown by the ball courts which appeared about A.D. 500 among the Hohokam. These influences in the medium of trade goods later reached the Anasazi. With them, of course, must have come new ideas and religious beliefs.

A full discussion of Pueblo myth and religious ceremonialism is wisely omitted in this already exhaustive, factual text, for myth exists in a different dimension of time and comprehension from rationalized history. It recounts the upward journey of the soul from the darkness of the unconscious into the light of consciousness, a path that cannot be time-tabled, that has left no earthly landmarks. The Creation Myth of the Hopis, for example, is far more than the primitively childish folktale we popularly imagine of mankind's emergence from inside the earth to its surface through a hole called the *sipapu*. It embraces a vast cosmological concept of three successive previous worlds, which is identical with those of the Creation Myths of the pre-Columbian Aztecs, Toltecs, and Mayas, and it is paralleled by the tenets of ancient Persian, Hindu, and Tibetan Buddhist religious philosophy. Upon it is still structured the present-day annual cycle of nine Hopi ceremonials, with their many separate rituals. That they have a deep psychological significance, akin to the findings of Jung's modern depth psychology, is beyond doubt. Little wonder that scholars of all nations, as well as hundreds of students and thousands of curious visitors, are seeking their subjective truths.

These remarks may not be as extraneous as they first seem if they suggest an inner life of an ancient people which needs to be plumbed as well as their outer life. They reaffirm my earlier comments that emerging primordial images are dictating in the present, as they dictated in the long past, mankind's ever-changing conception of the earth and its invisible forces. Who can doubt that we today are living in a myth of our own making, as did the Anasazi, and that someday they may coincide?

This, in short, is an evocative book. The sensitivity of its full-color photographic essays evokes the mystic beauty, the sublime terror, and ever-present mystery of this great nuclear heartland of America. And in proper balance the earthy objectivity of its text outlines the long span of the responsive Anasazi, who have bequeathed to us their heritage of the oldest, largest, and most beautiful monumental ruins in all America.

The People Who Have Vanished

In the plateau country of the American Southwest there stand sandstone monuments to a people's passage, the vestigial remains of a civilization that rose, flourished, and then disappeared. The ruins of great stone cities, crouched low on the mesa tops and nestled in caves along the sheer canyon walls of this high desert region, are the mute remnants of a world that completed its life cycle centuries before European man set foot on the shores of this continent.

Seen now it is a civilization rendered in earth tones, hued by the soft reds, ambers, rich loam browns, and bleached tans that are the natural condition in this land of wind and sun. Built with the rock and earth that lay readily at hand and hunkered close upon the rock from which they were born, the old cities have weathered well, retreating only slightly, and then only into a more harmonious union with the face of the land. They, like the earth, abide in a quiet strength, a presence that betokens an assurance of permanence, a surety of function—for they are memorials to the inventiveness of The People.

The People are gone, but their memory and the story of their passing survives in the great stone homes they built. What they called themselves we will never know, for they left no written records; like most primitive peoples, they probably chose the name which meant "The People," for such seems to be the nature of man's self-image. Surely they did not use the name by which we know them, *Anasazi* ("The Ancient Ones"), as the Navajo called them centuries later.

We know these people also by their deeds, for they were the cliff dwellers, the builders in stone, the ancient people of the rock. The great dwellings alone are sufficient testament to their achievements, but like the name, they are more mystery than solution, piquing the curiosity and tantalizing the imagination, leading to questions about the form and substance of Anasazi life. Though long dormant, they have patiently held the echoes of Anasazi life for those who would come close enough to listen.

On a bitterly cold December day in 1888, two cowboys chasing strays through the tangled canyons and mesas above the Mancos River in southwestern Colorado broke out along the rimrock to let their horses blow and get their bearings. Under leaden skies a shifting veil of light snow swayed and pulsed on the tentative currents and eddies of the wind, obscuring their view of the canyon below and adding to a growing suspicion that it was the wrong day to be outside looking for anything. But even as they rested, a decisive draft pushed between the canyon walls, sweeping the falling snow before it, to reveal what looked like a stone house—no, a whole series of stone houses—tucked back in a huge recess in the cliffs across from them.

There, alternately hidden and then haloed by the swirling snow, standing quiet and protected under the cap rock in the natural amphitheater that eons of seeping water had carved out of the cliff face, was a complex of rooms and towers bound together in a single mass of shaped and fitted sandstone that rose, curved, dipped, and squared with a grace and delicacy that seemed to mask its sheer bulk. The two men had heard talk from their Ute neighbors that there were Indian relics to be found on the mesa, but they were not prepared for anything like this.

They made their way down the steep ravine on improvised ladders and up the broken talus slope to stand at the foot of their discovery. Small windows stared vacantly past them as they probed along the front of the buildings and scuffed the dust of undisturbed centuries. Inside, they found clay pots, a stone axe, several skeletons, and sundry discards of a hasty departure; but taken altogether, they could not be sure of what they had found. All they really knew was that a people of considerable accomplishment had lived here once—and had vanished.

What Richard Wetherill and Charlie Mason found that December day was just one of many prehistoric Indian ruins that dot the Mesa Verde, all long abandoned. Their discovery was not the first sighting of a cliff dwelling in Mesa Verde, for as early as 1874 William H. Jackson, the famed photographer of the Hayden Survey, had photographed a ruin in Mancos Canyon. But Wetherill and Mason had found Cliff Palace, the glittering jewel of Mesa Verde, preserved and protected from the erosion of time by its cave. With the subsequent discoveries of Spruce Tree House, Square Tower House, and the scores of other ruins nested in the canyon walls, it rapidly became obvious that here had been the home of a large and highly developed civilization, now gone and apparently forgotten.

The Anasazi were builders and settlers on a large and permanent scale, and it is for this that they are best remembered. At a time many centuries before the European discovery and settlement of the Americas, the Anasazi had developed a complex civilization of large and closely related communities. They erected massive and multistoried apartment buildings, walled cities, and cliff dwellings of shaped and mortared sandstone. They were dedicated farmers who planted, tilled, and even irrigated their crops, putting by the harvest to see them through the year. They were creative craftsmen of pottery and jewelry, and practiced a highly formalized religion in distinctive ceremonial chambers. The permanence and stability that they saw in their lives was reflected in the homes they built, but for reasons not yet completely understood their civilization lacked the durability of their building. The Anasazi abandoned their homeland, leaving the great stone cities and familiar farmlands for other areas of the Southwest, eventually to mix in the amalgam of modern Pueblo.

The lifeway that was Anasazi began in what we know today as the Four Corners region—where the states of Utah, Colorado, New Mexico, and Arizona come together at a common point. It is high plateau country stretching in all directions across a broken and rolling landscape that rises with abrupt sandstone mesas jaggedly carved by the deep-cutting Colorado, Little Colorado, and San Juan rivers. The southern reaches of the plateau, down into west central New Mexico and east central Arizona, are dotted with the extensive lava flows and cinder deposits of volcanic activity.

Moisture is not abundant on the plateau, and with the exception of the large, permanent rivers, the areas where it collects are chiefly a result of altitude. Moisture-bearing clouds come from the southwest, borne on winds from the Gulf of California, and are pushed up to precipitate by the high mountains and mesas. There the water forms seasonal streams or seeps through the porous sandstone to collect and form tiny springs.

This pattern of precipitation has dictated in large measure the kinds of vegetation to be found on the plateau. Along the lower elevations, where water is generally more scarce, sagebrush and juniper are found to prevail, while the better-watered land above 6,000 feet might tend toward piñon and pine. A particular area favored by peculiar circumstances of moisture or temperature will break the pattern, creating a small concentration of normally high-altitude flora such as Douglas fir at an unlikely low altitude.

The same conditions of precipitation that dictate plant life also have a profound effect on man. Water is probably the single most important commodity in the arid and semiarid Southwest, and the earliest Indian settlers clustered close around rivers, springs, and high plateaus that promised enough water to nurture their crops.

The Anasazi found their water and built their civilization near the center of the plateau immediately surrounding the Four Corners, within the drainage basin of the San Juan River. In this region the Anasazi concentrated into three distinct and vigorous population centers at Chaco Canyon, Mesa Verde, and Kayenta. While Anasazi peoples would in time spread across the entire plateau, and the influence of their culture would reach out to affect the lives of almost every other prehistoric Indian civilization in the Southwest,

these cities would remain the most striking examples of what it meant to be Anasazi.

At Chaco Canyon, southeast of Four Corners, Anasazi reached great heights first. In the broad, long alluvial valley carved and deposited by the north fork of the Chaco Wash, they built Pueblo Bonito—eight hundred rooms covering more than three acres, reaching four and five stories high in places, nestled close against the sheer cliffs of the canyon wall but entirely freestanding. All along the canyon floor stand the ruins of other sizable pueblos, most no more than a twenty-minute trot apart, hinting at a loosely related citystate that numbered its population in the many thousands.

North and east of the Four Corners is Mesa Verde, where the art of building in the caves that sculpt the walls of the myriad canyons reached its highest levels. Originally the Anasazi of the Mesa Verde built freestanding pueblos in the open, but it is the cliff dwellings—built near the end of the Anasazi occupation of Mesa Verde—that provide the most inspiring spectacle for visitors. Preserved from the elements by the protective shelter of the caves, the cliff dwellings have survived the centuries largely intact. Above the cliffs, on the expanses between the canyons that inspired an early Spaniard of uncertain identity to name the region "Green Table," the Anasazi planted and tended their fields.

Among the rugged canyons and twisted ridges that rise toward Navajo Mountain in the southwest quadrant of the Four Corners is the Kayenta region, where Tsegi Canyon is probably typical of their architectural achievement. In Tsegi Canyon the builders worked their craft both in the caves, as at Betatakin, and in the open, as at Keet Seel, where cave dwellings and freestanding structures existed almost side by side. For reasons not precisely clear, the masons of Kayenta never reached the excellence in execution that marks the work of their kinsmen to the north and east.

For many years it was assumed by a number of archaeologists that the origins of the Anasazi were to be found in the Cochise Culture that preceded the other civilizations of southwestern prehistory, but this was difficult to prove because of a dearth of hard evidence. As a result, a hopeful blank space was left at the beginning of Anasazi chronologies, indicating that something must have been there. In the past several decades, conscientious digging has shown that the Anasazi did indeed grow from a Cochise root.

The Anasazi tradition itself can be divided into two parts: the earlier Basket Maker and the later Pueblo. The Basket Makers have been traced back in the San Juan region to about the time of Christ. They were so named, logically enough, because of the fine basketry they produced and because they had none of the pottery researchers had found in other, chronologically later archaeological sites. Many of the early Basket Makers lived in caves, although in some areas they began to build pithouses, a trend that would grow and spread. The pithouses were shallow, saucer-like dwellings, walled and roofed with a combination of logs and mud mortar. Until about A.D. 500 the Basket Makers moved within the San Juan region, dividing their time between hunting and cultivating a yellow flint corn.

About the year 500 changes began to appear in the Basket Maker pattern of life. The modifications were not abrupt but evolutionary and varied in time from place to place throughout the San Juan, but generally speaking, the mood of change was upon the Basket Makers about this time. In the broadest terms, they were becoming more sedentary; a greater dependence on agriculture was developing; pithouses were deepened and more permanently constructed to accommodate domestic activities and family ceremonies; and they began to build the circular, subterranean ceremonial structures that would become rigidly formalized as great kivas. They also began to make pottery, a skill apparently learned from neighbors to the south.

Toward the end of this period, nearing A.D.

700, they began to show signs of a dramatic cultural advancement. The bow and arrow made its appearance, displacing the less efficient atlatl and spear. Cotton weaving was introduced, and full-grooved axes suddenly were in use. All were signs of contact with other peoples, but the rapid acceptance of the new ways indicated that the Anasazi had an adaptable, inquisitive, and thoroughly dynamic culture.

The accomplishments of the Basket Maker Anasazi were extraordinary, but about A.D. 700 they began a transition in building techniques that earned them a new name, Pueblo, and changed the architectural modes of their Southwest neighbors. The Pueblo Anasazi built in stone and masonry, rising up to build on the surface and reserving subterranean structures for ceremonial purposes. Rapidly developing their skills as masons, the Anasazi first built a few contiguous rooms and later elaborated the style into multistoried warrens of rooms and plazas that served as cities.

Whatever the stimulus for all the change and growth, whether it came from within or without, the Anasazi multiplied the refinements in their cultural pattern dramatically during the ensuing centuries. Between about 900 and 1100, they began building some of their most impressive dwellings, raised pottery craftsmanship and decoration to hitherto unknown levels, indulged in a variety of craft arts, devoted a compelling amount of energy to religion and the construction of enormous kivas, and saw their influence spread across the entire Southwest, with certain tendrils of their culture reaching as far as southwest Texas and Nevada. Their culture spread almost intact into the Upper Rio Grande region and with slight modifications poured down over the Mogollon Rim to the mountains and deserts of central and southern Arizona to become the Sinagua and later Salado.

For two hundred years following this phenomenal florescence, the Anasazi consolidated their gains and settled down to enjoy the good life they had wrought. From roughly A.D. 1100 to 1300, the largest Pueblos were built, pottery in its most advanced forms was crafted, and the Anasazi lifeway seemed established. Some might argue that it had ceased to grow and that a culture which does not grow must necessarily begin to die. The question is largely moot, though, because before 1300 the Anasazi began to leave their homes—in some cases a full century before that date—until by 1300 the once great cities of the plateau were silent and vacant, drying in the Southwest winds like the husk of some long dead insect, retaining form but lacking the essence of a once active life.

Two plausible explanations exist for the Anasazi departure from a homeland where life was full and complete: either life had ceased to be good and they were starved out, or they were driven out by someone else. There are strong indications that a severe drought extended over the plateau from 1276 to 1299, and quite possibly the Anasazi found agriculture as they had come to depend on it impossible. There are subtle inconsistencies to the theory, however, that tend to impeach its universality, giving rise to the second possibility. Wandering Shoshonean hunters—raiders by nature—had begun to roam the plateau somewhat earlier, and given the fortresslike quality of most Anasazi pueblos and cliff dwellings, it seems possible that these raiders had begun to make part, or most, of their living by preying on the vulnerable fields of the agriculturists. If this was the case, the Anasazi would in time be forced out. Whatever the answer, and it may be a combination of both, the Anasazi departed to other regions.

Where they all went cannot be determined absolutely, but certainly some decamped to the upper and middle Rio Grande region, and others possibly formed or joined the pueblos at Ácoma, Laguna, Hopi, and Zuñi. Whatever their destinations, in the process of moving and of mixing with other peoples, the purity and vitality of the culture that had been Anasazi was seriously eroded.

The Anasazi are only a part of a greater, often interrelated story of Southwestern prehistory, which finds two other cultures—the Mogollon and Hohokam—exerting vast influences upon the people of the San Juan.

The mountain country of the Southwest that lies curved like a scimitar, cutting between the plateau and the desert from central Arizona to south central New Mexico, was the home of the Mogollon culture. The Mogollon peoples began to develop a sedentary culture several hundred years earlier than the Anasazi, building with rock, making pottery, crafting fine stone tools, and practicing religion more intensely. Quite probably it was the Mogollon example, coupled with Hohokam and Mexican influences picked up through trade contact, that accounted for the Anasazi cultural explosion about A.D. 900. Before long the Anasazi culture began to completely absorb and overshadow Mogollon, until by about 1000 it had ceased to exist as a distinct tradition.

Farther south and west, in the desert along the drainage of the Gila River, the Hohokam developed parallel with, but distinct from, the Mogollon. The Hohokam evolved as master irrigators, turning river waters through extensive canal systems to their crops. But more than that, they were the cultural conduit through which the trinkets, tools, and ideas of Mexico found their way north to the Anasazi. It was Hohokam, combined with Anasazi, that resulted in the distinctive Salado and Sinagua cultures that developed during the golden age of Hohokam.

The task of understanding what it was that Richard Wetherill and Charlie Mason had found in December of 1888 has often been frustrating and confusing, and it is not completely answered yet. But in the fewer than nine decades that have elapsed, an extraordinary amount of information has been squeezed from the dry and lifeless remnants that survive. The methods that have evolved for reading the story the Anasazi left buried and scattered behind them on their cultural climb and migrations are almost as extraordinary and ingenious as the accomplishments of the Anasazi.

The primary tool of the archaeologist is stratigraphy, that is, the study of strata, or levels, laid down in the course of a people's presence in one spot. The task is to pick through layers of junk that have been trampled underfoot or tossed on the trash heap, and from this examination to determine the relative sequence in which certain items were acquired, improved upon, and finally transcended by some other item. The study can extend to houses, tools, jewelry, clothing, food, pottery, or any item that will not decay. The study proceeds on the assumption that people do not normally dig down in the garbage to throw something away and that with only occasional exceptions, what is found on top is the most recent, what is found on the bottom is the oldest.

The shortcoming with stratigraphy is that it is relative, not absolute. Digging down may reveal that some individual quit bashing his neighbor with a dull club and started using a sharp one, but it won't tell the investigator *when* this momentous discovery occurred. Two methods were developed to bridge this gap—carbon-14 dating and dendrochronology. The first is a product of the nuclear age and functions because the amount of radiation emitted by carbon 14 diminishes at a regular rate once an organism dies. Therefore, by measuring the amount of radiation still present in an object, the approximate date of its death can be determined.

An even more exact method of absolute dating is dendrochronology, or the study of tree rings. Trees respond to the environment, particularly to the moisture available, very sensitively—and in certain types of trees this response is directly reflected in the layer of growth they add each year. It was found that different trees will show the same relative response to climate; once this was discovered, it became a matter of tracing the sequence back through a series of overlapping samples. Thus, a tree-ring sample of unknown date could be compared to one of known antiquity.

It took years to trace tree-ring dates back to a time useful in the study of the Anasazi, but now with dendrochronology a beam from a structure can be dated for the year when it was cut, which appreciably narrows the margin for error in dating a ruin.

Pottery has assumed a role of considerable importance in the evaluation of the development, spread, and influence of cultures. This is due in large measure to the fact that pottery does not decay or deteriorate over centuries of time, and even when broken, the shards are usually sufficient to supply requisite clues. Southwestern pottery becomes a useful tool in research because different prehistoric groups made pottery differently and chose to decorate 20 to 30 percent of their vessels with paints, slips, and glazes. By examining the materials used, techniques of manufacture, and the designs employed, specialists can trace where a pottery type originated, when it joined or diverged from other traditions, how new influences were introduced or assimilated, and how it may have evolved by itself. It is a lengthy process of analysis and comparison that often seems to border on the arcane, but it is one of the most useful tools for examining the interrelationships of peoples in the prehistoric Southwest.

The life cycle of Anasazi is a remarkable documentary of a people learning to cope with the world as they found it. In little more than thirteen centuries a people walked the long road from small bands of hunters and gatherers to great communities of farms and cities. From beginning to end they took the best and the worst that nature had to dish out, and they managed not only to survive, but also to grow and prosper. They were a people who borrowed the ideas, tools, and techniques of some, and in turn lent them to others. They learned the ways to a higher civilization and then embellished on those new ways themselves. Theirs is a story of success and of failure, of challenge, ingenuity, accomplishment, and even mystery and contradiction. It is, then, a very human story—of a people who left their ghosts among the rocks.

Unusual double mug from Mesa Verde.

MESA VERDE

By the arbitrary standards of modern political boundaries, it stands in the Colorado quadrant of the Four Corners region, but in mood and spirit it is still the heartland of Anasazi. Its name the legacy of some forgotten Spanish trader who saw this land rising out of the high desert as a tremendous Green Table, the Mesa Verde remains isolated and intact, the province of the ancient lifeway. It was a home to the Anasazi from that time when the earliest Basket Maker hollowed out a pithouse near his corn patch and laid the foundation for 1,300 years of civilization; and it continues to retain the spirit of those people because it was never really home to anyone else.

The Utes and Navajos who ranged the lands around the Mesa Verde during the centuries after the Anasazi departed left little trace of any continued residence on the mesa, and in time the Utes came to regard this land of ghostly ruins as a fearsome, unholy place. The Spaniards, interested in glory and the transplantation of Iberian civilization, never tarried long near this wilderness. Even the American cattle ranchers along the Mancos River, whose stock grazed into the mesa country, found the imposing bluffs and tangled canyons too challenging for any permanent settlement. Thus the Mesa Verde remained inviolate until the condition was codified in National Park status in 1906.

Their stamp is everywhere upon the land, the presence of Anasazi felt in every canyon where silent ruins grow out of the sandstone bluffs, and the ghosts of ancient farmers materialize in stray sounds tossed by the winds that course across the mesa tops. They were a peaceful, industrious people with roots wound deep in generations of life upon the land—a people who had grown to be a part of the land, moving in harmony to the orchestrated order that Nature laid down with the seasons. Theirs was the life discovered in living; the sense of being, discovered in believing; the sense of beauty, discovered in the balance and renewal of the world.

Overleaf: Cliff Palace, protected under an imposing brow of sandstone, was once the golden home of hundreds of Mesa Verde Anasazi. Now it harbors only parties of awestruck tourists.

24

*Village life as it may have developed among the Anasazi
is re-created in dioramas at Mesa Verde National Park:
the simplicity of early Basket Maker life (lower left);
a Modified Basket Maker village (near left); and community
life on the rooftops and the evolution of the
square kiva in the Developmental Pueblo era (far left).*

*In Classic Pueblo times life was marked by a sense of belonging;
women practiced the hearthside arts, young men labored to raise
corn and build cities, and old men basked in the sun.*

Clinging to the slope of the sandstone cave from which they were born, the walls and square tower of Cliff Palace meld this home of the Ancient Ones with the eternal rock. An often crude and poorly finished stonework, symptomatic of the Anasazi's hasty retreat to the cliffs, stands in contrast to the graceful overall design.

Fibers stripped from the long, tough stalks of the broad-leafed yucca were woven into sandals or wound together to make a cord that bound cloaks, nets, and roofbeams.

Winter aperture at Cliff Palace:
Protected from the direct onslaught
of wind and snow by its natural
sandstone shroud, the home of the
Anasazi waited out the quiet
months when the earth died—and
all suffered the cold and pain of
that death, clinging to the hope of
an early rebirth with the spring.

29

Corn was the staple of the Anasazi diet, whether green,
ripe, or as here, dried. In the dry Southwest climate it
would keep for years. When ground into a flour, it could
be served up as flat baked breads or dough balls
boiled in a stew.

The ancient rooms of Spruce Tree House, with sometimes
three stories squeezed under the cantilevered sandstone
ceiling, reach back deep into the cave. In front, with
ladders jutting from their entrances, are the kivas, whose
stone roofs saw further duty as a village plaza.

Mug House, under the lip of Wetherill Mesa: A kiva, its roof long since a victim of the ages, dominates the visual scene as it once did the spiritual life of the village. Opposite: Witnesses to the last flowering of Anasazi culture, the windows of Mug House stare in mute remembrance of those long departed days.

Through this characteristic T-shaped doorway at Mug House passed a people at once highly spiritual and solidly pragmatic. While easily defended, less drafty, and more convenient to enter with a load on one's back, these openings may nevertheless have been designed in response to religious rather than practical considerations.

Justifying its name, Long House stretches in a sweeping arc across the base of Wetherill Mesa.

Winter settles down around the home of the ancients at Spruce Tree House with a quiet
that conjures up shadows of forgotten ancestors for all who pass by.

Greening under the gentle but inexorable hand of spring, Long House stands alone to celebrate the
re-emergence of life in an amphitheater that once rang with the activity of a new year.

Spring House, an unexcavated ruin on Mesa Verde, still awaits the probing hand of twentieth-century man. Many ruins are left undisturbed by archaeologists in the hope that future researchers will develop new techniques to extract more information than is now possible.

The uncomplicated artistry of Mesa Verde potters is reflected in the bold simplicity of a double-handled canteen.

"Face of the Ancients" one might entitle this view of Balcony House, a probably unintended visage that reaches back nearly a thousand years.

On top of the mesa opposite Cliff Palace stands the Sun Temple, now shrouded in a regrowth of timber and brush, its original purpose still further obscured. Experts surmise a ceremonial function for it, but details of how and why are left to the imaginations of those who encounter it.

The petroglyphs of Navajo Canyon at Mesa Verde tell a muraled saga of a people's passage. In immortal stone they celebrate the triumphs of mortals in the hunt, in conflict, and in communication with the supernatural—all signed with a hand.

Square Tower House at Mesa Verde, nestled in the curving palm of the earth.
Villages grew by stages, testing the limits allowed by the land.

Out of the Earth

In the beginning there was the Creator, Tawa, who ruled over a domain of endless space and time and whose power was the source of all life, the Sun. He created the stars and planets of the universe to give dimension and substance to his realm, and deep within the Earth he placed the ant and insect creatures to inhabit this world. But the creatures fought among themselves and did not understand the meaning of life, so Tawa sent his emissary, the Spider Grandmother, to show the creatures the way to a new world where they might live in the way he wanted.

The Spider Grandmother led the creatures up from their old world to the new one Tawa had created for them closer to the surface of the Earth. As they emerged, the creatures found their bodies had changed, and they had the form of the bear, the wolf, the rabbit, and all the other furry animals. But here, too, they fell to fighting and killing among themselves, and still they did not understand the meaning of life. This was not what Tawa wanted of his creation, so once again the Spider Grand-

mother was dispatched to show the way.

The Spider Grandmother gathered the creatures about her and led them upward to a third world that lay just below the surface of the earth. Here the creatures had the form of man, and they spread out across the new world to plant their corn and live with peace, friendship, and reverence for the gods, as the Spider Grandmother had instructed them. For a time all was as Tawa wished, but among the people were sorcerers, who began leading them away from the original teachings, until the people spent all their time gambling, stealing, or fighting, and none of it working or practicing the rituals they had been taught. But some of the people continued to work, and make offerings of prayer sticks, and sing the songs that were necessary to leading a good life.

All this Tawa saw, and he sent the Spider Grandmother to bring the people of good heart who understood the meaning of life out of the third world grown iniquitous. Spider Grandmother led the chosen people upward toward

43

a small opening at the top of the third world and through the hole—known as *sipapu*—to the surface of the Earth. As they emerged, Mockingbird sat by Spider Grandmother and divided them into groups—Hopi, Zuñi, Pima, White Man, and all the other tribes of the world—sending each in its direction to follow life as Tawa had prescribed among the plains, rivers, and forests he had created for them.

Such was the genesis of man in the New World according to the Hopi, one of the descendent groups of the Anasazi. Told in all its detail, riddled with the wit and caprice of gods tinkering with man's perfectability, and the elation and despair of people learning to live with each other and their new world, it is an epic tale of man's presence and accomplishments in the Southwest. But for the men who root in the trash heaps and domestic ruin of the unrecorded past, it is a pale reckoning alongside the rich story of migration, cultural change, and development that the people who actually passed this way left behind.

The beginnings of the story can be seen in only the fuzziest outlines—faded glimpses of actors fleeting across a stage kept dim by eons of time and the circumstances of their lives—but enough can be seen to whet the imagination to an edge sufficiently keen to hew deeper for answers. It is known with almost complete certainty that man did not evolve in the Americas, but that he appeared in the full bloom of *homo sapiens*. Where he came from has been a subject of tireless inquiry, with some of the conclusions rivaling creation myths in their speculative derring-do and manipulation of plausibility. The possibility of ocean crossings from east or west is strongly augured against by the fact that man's presence is known in the Americas at least 13,000 years ago, and the shipbuilding technology in Asia, Europe, or Africa that long ago was not up to the challenge of the open sea for hundred-day-long voyages.

The proposal which currently does the least

violence to the evidence at hand is that man first made his way to North America from Asia, via the Bering Strait. The geological record indicates that between 25,000 and 11,000 years ago a land bridge existed in the strait, and that during this time there were periods when the climate was mild enough for man to endure the journey across. Even during the eras of relatively temperate weather, though, the northern climate was severe enough to dictate that our Odysseus had to have a hunter's temper and an arctic background to accompany his fiddle-foot.

Once in North America, the travelers of the long spear made their way inland, down the central plains of Canada, spreading out across the wide drainage of the Mississippi, and finally into the Southwest. It was a process that took centuries, and it was not the product of a single migration, but rather a case of numerous groups crossing the strait in succession. Physical characteristics of American Indians suggest that the earliest migrations were not made by people of a single racial or physical type, although later arrivals were of an increasingly Mongoloid stock.

Whatever the exact circumstances, by about 10,000 B.C. man was firmly entrenched in the Southwest, where a distinctive culture began to emerge. In the course of several thousand years, the hunters of the Southwest achieved a subtle shift in the way they filled their stomachs, and that difference would earn them the title of Desert culture, or Cochise, as the culture is regionally applied to the Southwest. As hunters they had found their daily bread (as their brethren on the plains to the east would continue to do) by waylaying mastodon, tapir, long-horned buffalo, and sundry smaller animals, occasionally supplementing their diet with seeds and berries they stumbled across in the course of the hunt. As Cochise Culture, the situation was reversed, for they devoted their energies to gathering seeds and plants, and dropped meat into the pot on an irregular basis. They were still a nomadic people, following the harvest as nature prescribed, but they were moving a little more slowly than the hunters—leaving a slightly more visible trail.

Fortunately for us, the people of the Cochise Culture occasionally took to the caves, building grass beds in these natural shelters and dumping their garbage in readily discovered heaps protected from the elements, where it could survive to be dug up and examined by several generations of a nosy twentieth century. By roughly 7,000 B.C. they had acquired the fire drill and developed the *metate*—the troughlike stone in which seeds and roots were ground into flour. In time they began making baskets, mats, and nets from woven plant fibers and furry blankets from the skins of rabbits they caught in their nets. It was a simple life, not a great deal different from that led by the hunters (especially in terms of tools and technology), but the emphasis upon plants for subsistence made the transition to agriculture a natural and welcome change when corn was finally introduced.

About 2,000 B.C. corn found its way into the Southwest—undoubtedly coming up the long chain of trade from southern Mexico, where it originated—to change the lives of some Cochise peoples gradually but irrevocably. The full impact of corn and agriculture on the Southwest would not be realized until shortly before the time of Christ, and then only regionally; in the south-central region, home of the Mogollon and Hohokam, the changes came earliest—a story to be told in the following chapter. Farther north, along the drainage of the San Juan River around the Four Corners region, in the cradle of the lifeway we call Anasazi, events were proceeding on a more gradual course.

The earliest Anasazi were the Basket Makers of the San Juan region, but any roots of the family tree running back further in time have been slow and difficult to unearth. The Basket Makers who appeared as a recognizable culture in the San Juan shortly after A.D. 1 shared enough traits in common with known Cochise types to lead archaeologists to suspect a connection. It is only during the last few decades that evidence has been found directly linking Cochise to Basket Maker in a transitional cultural overlap.

The Basket Makers who evolved on the plateau were a dynamic group suspended in the transition between simple hunters and gatherers and the sedentary life of full-time agriculturists. Between about A.D. 1 and 500, they subsisted between two worlds, gradually growing toward the life that offered the greatest security. They were seminomadic, chasing the natural bounty, but they knew the secrets of corn and squash—knowledge that demanded their presence in a single place for long periods of time.

Because of their often nomadic life-style, the Basket Makers were initially not great builders of permanent dwellings. Home was often a cave, with possibly occasional temporary shelters built in the open, of which no trace remains today. Nests were constructed in the backs of caves, shallow depressions behind a windbreak of rocks and logs, and lined with leaves or shredded bark for comfort and for warmth.

Impermanence was the rule, but in some of the caves can be found elaborate slab-lined cists. The cists were carefully constructed circular holes dug in the loose fill of the caves, sometimes six feet in diameter and two feet deep, and lined with flat rocks fitted to prevent the sides from collapsing. Food, seed corn, and household items were apparently stored in them and carefully covered to await the return of the Basket Maker family when they passed this way again in the course of their annual ramblings.

Some Basket Makers also began to construct pithouses, although the practice was apparently not universally understood or accepted. Among the best examples of this style are the pithouses to be found in the vicinity of Durango, Colorado. As early as A.D. 100 Basket Makers here scooped out shallow, saucer-shaped holes in the open that ranged in size from eight to twenty-five feet in diameter,

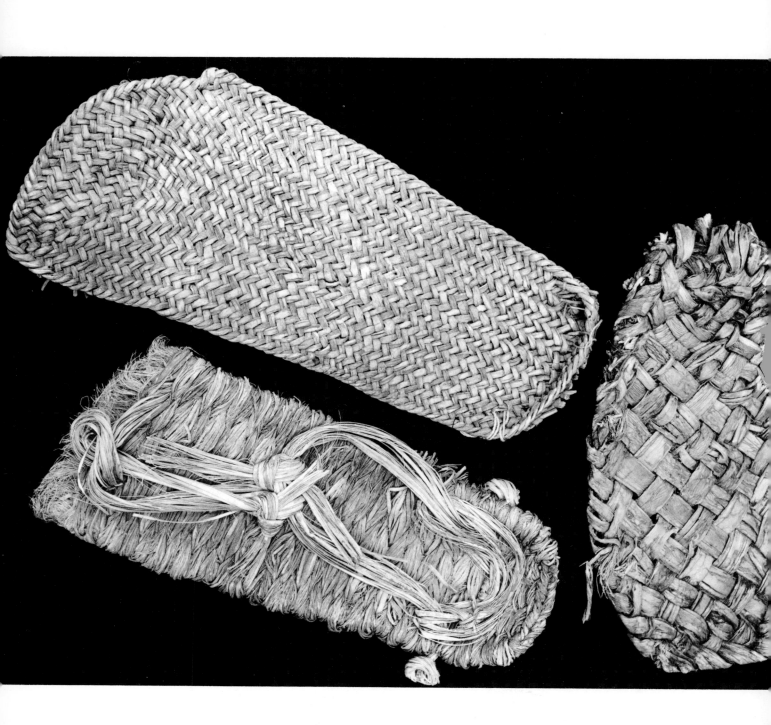

Sandals found at Basket Maker sites show the functional designs, variety, and craftsmanship
of which these early people were capable. Closely woven of yucca and apocynum fibers,
this footwear afforded good protection from the rocks, heat, and cactus of the desert floor.

with most tending toward the smaller size. The floors were normally clay-lined and often had storage cists hollowed into them. The walls were apparently of cribbed logs packed with a mud mortar, and roofed with logs from wall to wall with no supports rising from the center of the floor. Entrance was gained by an opening in the side, with no ventilator or smoke holes in evidence. Very possibly these pithouses did not contain firepits, but rather were heated with rocks brought from a fire outside the dwelling and placed in a heating pit in the floor. Although the occurrence of early pithouses was not generally widespread, some investigators are inclined to speculate that Basket Makers often built pithouses, using the caves for storage or only when they traveled, and that any other homes have simply been lost to the plateau's soil and weather.

But whatever the facts of their houses, it is the storage cists tucked deep in the caves that have the most to tell about the Basket Makers. It is here, in forgotten caches, that the food and implements of a shadow people have been found in greatest abundance, and here, too, that some of the Basket Makers themselves have turned up.

These early people of the plateau sometimes buried their dead in the slab-lined cists of the caves, the body flexed with knees and arms pulled tightly to the chest, wrapped in a blanket and accompanied on the long journey by new sandals, baskets, jewelry, and other necessities for a new life. The high, dry air of the plateau is often kind to perishables, drying rather than decaying; and as mummies huddled with a few prized possessions, some Basket Makers have survived through almost a score of centuries.

They were a short, stocky people, heavy-boned and long-headed, with hair that often defied the Mongoloid and Amerindian stereotype of straight and black by being lighter in color and exhibiting a tendency toward waviness. The men generally wore their hair long, while the women bobbed theirs—undoubtedly for fashion as well as utility. By contemporary standards, and most certainly by their own, they were a very attractive people.

As the name would suggest, they were basketmakers of an extraordinary talent. Using the long sturdy fibers of the yucca and apocynum (a plant related to milkweed), they fashioned shallow trays, flat-bottomed bowls, long conical baskets to carry water and food great distances, and even large suitcaselike trunks for storage. The finer baskets of tighter weave were made using the coiling technique, in which a bundle of grasses stiffened with slightly flexible rods was wound around and around, each coil rising above the next, and laced to the one below as the coiling progressed by a wide, continuous splint. The sewing splints were often dyed red and black, yielding decorative patterns in red, black, and white on the finished product. Looser-weave vessels were made by twining; numerous rods radiating out from the center of the basket like wagon spokes were laced between with long fibers in a circular fashion.

In the absence of pots, food had to be either roasted over an open fire or boiled in pitch-coated or tightly woven baskets. Since baskets would be burned in an open fire, the water was heated by dropping hot rocks from the fire into the water-filled baskets—a long and laborious task that usually left dinner highly seasoned with ashes.

Also woven from the yucca and apocynum fibers were sandals, an absolute necessity among the rocks and thorns of the Basket Maker homeland. They made two grades of footgear, generally: a rough-finished work shoe built up from whole or shredded yucca leaves and woven crosswise with long fibers, or a finely twilled sandal, often complete with buckskin fringe across the toe, for use on more formal occasions. In either case the sandals were square-toed and secured at the toe and heel by twine thongs.

During the warm months of the year they usually wore little more than their sandals and short fiber aprons, or gee strings, but the winds and snows of winter dictated something more substantial for protection from the cold. The Basket Makers responded with fur blankets and mantles. The raw material was supplied, albeit reluctantly, by the ubiquitous rabbit, whose skin was cut into long strips and wound around fiber cords to make full, furry ropes. These ropes were then laced together by more twine to yield a loosely woven but comfortably warm winter robe.

The rabbits who provided warmth for both the skin and the belly of the Basket Makers were often hunted communally, in large drives. Nets were fashioned, again of yucca fibers, with the addition of human hairs woven throughout—apparently the contribution of fashion-conscious women of the group. These nets, sometimes reaching 200 feet long and 3 or 4 feet wide, were stretched across washes and narrow canyons, and the rabbits were stampeded into them, where the hungry or cold hunters wielded their clubs with the most devastating effectiveness.

They hunted bigger game as well, on the scale of deer and mountain sheep, and for these the Basket Makers laid aside their nets and took up the atlatl. This was a spear thrower, the logical extension of a man's arm, that gave greater power and range to the hunter. The atlatl was nothing more than a flat stick, notched at one end to receive the butt of the spear, with finger loops near the other end for the hunter to grasp. As the prey was approached, the hunter would notch his spear, laying it along the top of the atlatl. Putting his first two fingers through the loops and balancing the spear with the remaining fingers, he would rise to full height, pull his arm back until the spear lay the full length of the atlatl and arm, and let fly. The atlatl spear was vastly superior to the hand-thrown spear, but difficult to control and infinitely inferior to the later bow and arrow. Still, it was the best they had, and they made do.

The farming technology of the Basket Makers was of even a lower level. Corn was planted with a sharp stick, a number of kernels in each hole, buried to a depth of a foot or more to take advantage of what little ground moisture existed. Any tilling or weeding done as the plants grew was accomplished with sticks shaped to a narrow blade on the digging end. This lack of sophisticated tools is to be expected, however; they were not farmers who depended on their crops for survival, but hunters and gatherers who indulged in agriculture as a novel sideline.

They were a people of the earth, taking what nature had to offer and not proposing to change the order of things. The land was their world; and they lived with and by the earth from which they had seemed to spring.

Schematic designs on a Kayenta olla.

KAYENTA

The region known as Kayenta stands on the western flank of the San Juan cradle land of Anasazi. With Mesa Verde and Chaco Canyon, it forms the triumvirate of core areas that spawned and nurtured the lifeway that eventually reached out to affect nearly all the prehistoric farmers in the Southwest. And to say Kayenta is to say Tsegi Canyon, for it was in this sinuous canyon country that the Anasazi gathered to raise their civilization.

It is a bare-bones land of little water, where stunted piñon and juniper predominate and the moist pocket of quaking aspen at Betatakin strike a dissonantly verdant note. As a whole, it was a land which supported a relatively smaller population than the other core areas, but during the culminant period it was a population that concentrated in large villages at the three key centers of Betatakin, Keet Seel, and Inscription House. The Anasazi who gathered at Keet Seel were sufficient to build the largest cliff dwelling in Arizona.

Among the world of the Anasazi, Kayenta constituted what seems now to have been a quiet backwater of cultural growth. The sophisticated innovations of Mesa Verde and Chaco were adopted slowly and deliberately, the people absorbing possibly more than they originated. With a charming disregard for the diction that "newer is better," they mixed the old building technique of wattle-and-daub with the more advanced pure stone masonry, continued to live in freestanding pueblos right next to the cliff dwelling at Keet Seel, and took their religion in smaller doses, avoiding the compulsive kiva-building that characterized Chaco especially. They were not lethargic bumpkins, country cousins to the true way; rather they were people faced with survival in a harder land, devoting their energies to the demands of the digging stick and the hunt, fulfilling the basic needs of life first, and adding the veneer and filigree of civilization as time permitted.

*Life in the round, no actors on the stage—the great ruin of Betatakin
echoes with the hollow sound of 150 abandoned rooms, a set
left over from a seven-hundred-year-old drama.*

*Alive with autumn color, Betatakin Canyon in Navajo National Monument lies in the heart of the
Kayenta region—a land of small streams, narrow canyons, and the unifying force of the rock.*

*The shape of life within a Kayenta cliff dwelling—hearthside chores
that were suddenly and finally interrupted—re-created here in
a visitor display at Navajo National Monument.*

*Diminished almost to insignificance by the size and grandeur of a landscape
that often traffics in overstatement, the dwellings of Betatakin
find stature by becoming a part of the whole.*

At Betatakin (which means "Hillside House") the Anasazi became as one with the rock, seeking out every available shelf and niche, no matter how precarious, to stake their claim as a living part of the land.

A Kayenta olla, though an everyday item for storing water or grain, blossomed as an extension of the artistry and skill of its maker.

Cliff dwellings at Keet Seel, eight miles up a branch canyon from Betatakin, represent the culmination of a borrowing culture, where stone construction meets wattle-and-daub, and pueblos built in the open stand an arrow's flight from sheltered cave dwellings.

Above and overleaf: Keet Seel, a village and a lifeway carved from the old rock.

Inscription House in Navajo National Monument, perched stolidly above a canyon floor of undulating rock and brush, is gradually giving way to the relentless toll of the elements.

Petroglyphs in Tsegi Canyon: Whether for religious or secular reasons, the Anasazi obeyed their urge to record in a timeless shout of "I am!" and thereby reserved their place in the known community of man.

Fragments of winters long passed from memory: Potsherds more durable than the mortals who made them challenge those who follow to gather the pieces and reconstruct the whole—to find what time has pulled apart, and perhaps to experience what it meant to be Anasazi.

The skeletal remains of a civilization that thrived and passed on centuries before the Americas were "discovered" still stand like a faithful sentinel over the old plazas and fields of Longhouse Valley in the Kayenta district.

*Petroglyphs chipped into the dark patina of an exposed rock
in the Painted Desert, Petrified Forest National Park,
encode some story of the past.*

Wind from
the South

The winds that nurture life in the Southwest rise from the south, pushing across the Pacific Ocean, the Gulf of California, and the Gulf of Mexico, gathering moisture in the growing folds of the clouds that clothe the winds. Bearing northward, laden with the water that means life to an otherwise arid land, they sweep across the desert and mountains to leave a part of their cargo on the plateau homeland of the Anasazi. Sometimes the ration is deficient, and the land and its creatures shrink with the pinch; occasionally, just to be contrary, there is too much all at once, and the land rumbles and shakes with rampaging flash floods. But usually there is just barely enough to succor—and carry through to the next rain—those that agree to live by the dictates of the land and its capricious elements.

And so it was for the Anasazi. In time, especially as they turned more and more to agriculture, they lived and prospered or languished according to the beneficence of the winds from the south. But for the lifeway that

was Anasazi there was more coming north than just the rains: there were the ideas and innovations of men, developing in the mountains and desert of the south, that would feed and nourish life on the plateau as surely as a spring rain.

At a time when the Basket Makers were laying the foundations of Anasazi in the bedrock of the plateau, far away to the south the Mogollon and Hohokam peoples were already raising the walls of singular civilizations. Amid the mountains that flank the Mogollon Rim's sweeping arc across the heart of the Southwest, the people we now call Mogollon were living a sedentary life of permanent houses and agriculture fully two centuries before the Basket Makers slowed their ramblings enough to leave a trace of their passing. South and west of the mountains, in the flat desert lands, the Hohokam—a name settled on them by their Pima descendants, meaning "Those Who Have Vanished"—were gathered along the river banks near the confluence of the Gila and the Salt, where they would in time turn the arid land to their will with irrigation.

They were peoples further advanced than the Basket Makers, and to a certain degree they shared the blueprints of culture, loaning the tools and ideas that are the binding mortar of every civilization. Under the stimulus of these mentors to the south, the Anasazi would develop a dynamic and vigorous culture that would finally come rolling back to reshape the lives of Mogollon and Hohokam alike.

The people that we know as Mogollon and Hohokam also had their beginnings deep in the Cochise variant of the Desert Culture. They were archetypal examples of the hunters and gatherers of the Southwest, who found their lives being changed by the introduction of corn, beans, and squash. Much earlier than the Basket Makers—possibly by as much as several hundred years—the Cochise forebears of Mogollon and Hohokam began to slow their wanderings, settling longer at fewer camps, inexorably accommodating themselves to the spring and summer growth cycle of their crops. And with the surplus of the harvest dried and stored away, they no longer were obliged to spend the entire winter chasing today's, and sometimes yesterday's, dinner toward a chilly horizon.

As Cochise, the people of the mountains and desert showed a striking similarity to each other in their response to the challenge of survival in the Southwest, to the point where they are virtually indistinguishable. But in time new innovations appeared that were natural outgrowths of the sedentary agricultural life these people had adopted, most notably permanent houses, ceremonial dwellings, and pottery. And it was in the elaboration upon these innovations that the Mogollon and Hohokam distinguished themselves from each other—and left the cultural toddling of Cochise behind them. They were not a different people, of altered racial stock, but simply a culture grown into a new name, bifurcating at the touch of imagination and need between mountain and desert.

It was the Mogollon of the mountain country who developed first and fastest. During the two centuries before the birth of Christ, a proto-Mogollon people began to appear, still carrying the cultural baggage of Cochise but gradually developing in isolated areas of ingenuity the homes and pottery that would mark them as Mogollon. Throughout the mountainous drainages of the upper Gila and Salt rivers, the early Mogollon planted and tilled their corn, beans, and squash with the traditional—and marginally efficient—digging stick. They continued to hunt with the atlatl-thrown spear, although late in the period the bow and arrow would appear. Baskets, made by very nearly the same techniques and with many of the same materials as the Basket Makers employed, provided most of the vessels for cooking and storage. Wickerwork also provided essential sandals and mats, although an occasional pacesetter fashioned moccasins out of animal skins. They were apparently a friendly sort who got on well with their neighbors, for conspicuous among their trinkets and jewelry are bracelets made of seashells, hinting rather broadly that they were participants in a chain of trade stretching south and west to Pacific waters.

The Mogollon enjoyed a secure existence, reaping the natural benefits of life in a region of rich soils, plentiful water, and abundant game. The quality of that life would improve with the introduction of such amenities as pottery, the bow and arrow, and permanent houses. By their own hand and the healthy injection of new concepts and techniques from Mexico, the Mogollon would make a good life even better.

Pottery appeared among the Mogollon rather suddenly, in the sense that there were few of the groping crudities that normally accompany such an epoch-making technological advance. As early as 200 B.C. at least one Mogollon housewife was rejoicing over the wonders of this marvelous new vessel that didn't leak, didn't burn up, and let her boil water without tossing ash-frosted rocks into

*Like their Mogollon and Hohokam neighbors to the south, Anasazi farmers learned
to make the most of the few precious inches of rain that fell on their mesas.*

the pot. The discovery took time to spread throughout the range of the Mogollon, but within a two-hundred-year span most of the mountain folk were enjoying its benefits.

It was once postulated that the secret to making pottery was discovered by a careless cook. The notion holds a pleasing plausibility, inasmuch as during pre-pottery days it was often the practice to line the shallow parching baskets with clay and allow it to sun-dry. A clay-lined basket left too near a fire might ignite, burn away the basket, fire the clay in the process, and *voilà*, a pot. Although some later Anasazi pots created this way had a certain durability, experimentation has shown that, in most instances, such pots are either not thoroughly baked or crumble to pieces when touched.

More than likely, the first Mogollon potter learned the skill from an outsider. Far away to the south, in central and southern Mexico, the craft had reached a high order many centuries before pottery appeared among any of the Southwest Indians. Because the Mogollon —and all the early people of the Southwest, for that matter—were gregarious traders, it would only be natural for the knowledge to make its way north with other trade items. Consistent with this is the fact that pottery of a high order was made almost from the beginning, with virtually no fumbling stages in its evolution.

"High order" is a relative expression, for while the technique was adequate and thorough, the early pots did not approach the aesthetic levels of later work. The pottery was undecorated and often not smoothly finished, ranging in color from a dull buff to a reddish-brown. The vessels were shaped into bowls and small jugs, but most common were larger, narrow-necked jars that replaced leaky baskets for carrying and storing water. These large jars also provided stored grains and seed corn with maximum protection from mildew and bugs.

Because of their obvious superiority over baskets, the Mogollon woman settled herself to the task of making pottery at every oppor-

tunity. She used a method we now distinguish as "coil-and-scrape," although she knew it only as the method her mother had taught her and *the* way to make pots. She fashioned long cylinders of clay and began coiling in a continuous loop, gradually raising her vessel coil by coil in the approximate shape she wanted. This done, she began scraping the surface with a small stone or a shard from a broken pot, smoothing the coils to a flat surface and shaping the bowl as she finally wanted it. She fired over a bed of coals burned down from wood or dried dung, probably inverting the vessel, and then carefully piling more wood or dung around the bowl, leaving room for the air to circulate.

This latter aspect is important, for fresh air mixing with the heat creates an oxidizing atmosphere. The iron naturally present in the clay, when oxidized, emerges from the firing as yellow, orange, or red, depending on the percentage of iron involved. When the Mogollon began decorating their pottery between A.D. 1 and 500—first the inside of bowls and later the outside of narrow-mouthed vessels— they applied slips of high-iron-content clay thinned with water, carefully smoothed on, and later polished. The predominant decorations were repeating geometric designs, created by using straight lines of a rich burnished red on the pot. In addition to the slipped and polished ware, the Mogollon also established a parallel tradition of red-on-brown pottery, in which unpolished red designs were painted on the unslipped brown surface before firing.

But pottery was not the only innovation to touch the lives of the Mogollon. At about the time pottery began to make life easier for the women, the bow and arrow appeared in the hands of the men. The bow and arrow did not originate with the Mogollon, but as with pottery, they were the first Indians of the Southwest to have it. Again like pottery, the bow and arrow probably came up from the south—at least it was present in Mexico during pre-Mogollon times.

To every people in the history of mankind, the bow and arrow has been an important acquisition. It fired a projectile farther, faster, and harder than any spear could be thrown, with the added advantage that it could be used with full effectiveness while crouching or peeking around rocks and trees. No longer would the quarry enjoy a handicap of two leaps while man stood and reared back to throw.

For the Mogollon in particular it was a great step forward. The mountains and valleys of their home were the year-round range of more game than anywhere else in the Southwest, and despite the increasing dependence on agriculture, the Mogollon continued to be avid hunters. Curiously, they retained a stubborn attachment to the atlatl, using it in addition to the bow and arrow until well after A.D. 1000. Perhaps they just enjoyed the security of a good, stout short-range magnum.

The Mogollon were also the first of the Southwest cultures to begin building houses of any permanence. Unlike pottery and the bow and arrow, architecture was probably not the legacy of some messiah from the south, but was conceived and developed by the Mogollon themselves. Before A.D. 100 they had begun building circular pithouses in the open, scooping out a hole several feet deep, piling up low sidewalls reinforced with poles and brush, and erecting a single center post to support a conical roof. A short, sloping entryway on one side of the pithouse served as a door, and there was probably a hole in the center of the roof to accommodate a centrally located firepit. Storage pits for jars and baskets of food and seed corn were also dug into the floor and later into the sidewalls.

From the beginning, groups of Mogollon who clustered together to build pithouses generally carved out one extra dwelling, much deeper and larger (often reaching thirty to thirty-five feet in diameter) but constructed along the same pattern as the houses. It was their ceremonial house, the earliest of the great kivas, where a people went to dance on the floor drums that ringed the perimeter, sing the songs of their ancestors, and make certain that they were in harmony with the awesome forces of nature.

Although the houses grew bigger, deeper, and more elaborate with time, the Mogollon clung to the general design of a circular pithouse and sloping entry until about A.D. 700. Then influences from the Hohokam began to reshape the houses as square, then rectangular, and finally a new style altogether appeared about A.D. 1000, with the arrival of the Anasazi example. And this was really the quintessence of the Mogollon story.

Throughout the Southwest they were uniformly the first with the most: in pottery, in armament, and in houses. From A.D. 1 to about 500, they developed and refined their pottery and their houses. Between about 500 and 700, they were imitated throughout the mountains and into much of the plateau and desert country. But they never did any more than refine—they never evolved. In time they were left standing, first by the Hohokam and later by the Anasazi, until *they* became the imitators and the Mogollon culture as a separate entity ceased to exist.

What they had found, they kept, and they used it very well. They were a source of inspiration in some measure to both the Hohokam and Anasazi, but when they lost their dynamic growth, Mogollon began to die. Very probably this cultural lethargy was caused by the conditions of their lives: there was plenty of rain, so the corn grew well and abundantly; the forests were rich in game for the taking; and they were isolated from any kind of outside threat by the rugged mountain terrain. It was a good life—why change it? And so they didn't.

Not long after the Mogollon began their cultural rise, maybe no more than a hundred years later, the desert people to the southwest of the mountains began the process of development and cultural coalescence that became Hohokam. Although they came from the same Cochise root as the Mogollon—in fact the pre-Mogollon and pre-Hohokam peoples were practically indistinguishable—they would develop more slowly and deliberately than Mogollon and ultimately evolve a distinct, dynamic, and more enduring lifeway.

For all their accomplishments, and they were considerable, the Hohokam have been the nemesis of archaeologists. Because there were few trees in the desert with which to build, the Hohokam stymied efforts at dendrochronology (tree-ring dating) by leaving precious few timbers in abandoned houses. As if to thwart further poking into their affairs, the Hohokam cremated their dead and broke the bones, thereby leaving no anatomical trace. And as if that were not enough, they broke the pottery and stone burial offerings, usually a rich source of information, before interring the ashes (perhaps they were simply a singularly pragmatic people and sent a departed soul on its way with goods already broken and therefore no longer useful to the living).

During their early years the Hohokam left a confusing and often blind trail of their activities. Sometime before A.D. 100 and possibly much earlier, they learned to make pottery, either from their Mogollon neighbors or via Mexico, a possibility supported by later evidence of strong and direct influences from Mexico in other crafts. Whatever the source, the Hohokam produced a pottery that shared some characteristics with that of the Mogollon.

The Hohokam fired their pottery using the oxidizing technique, and consequently their early decorated ware ran predominantly to reds and buffs. But in time their decoration of the pots became more elaborate than that of the Mogollon. The Hohokam tended toward intricate blocked and rectangular geometric designs and graceful repeating scrolls that wrapped the vessel in the dazzling weave of the potter's imagination. The Hohokam also made greater use of vegetable paints (a technique also known to the Mogollon) during later stages of development. The carbon in the slips made from plants, when treated to an oxygen-rich firing, rendered itself as a strong black. Pottery design varied regionally and temporally for the Hohokam—as it did for Mogollon and Anasazi—and the variations in

color combinations from black through gray, and buff, yellow, orange, and red fairly boggles the imagination.

Despite the similarity in firing methods, the Hohokam added their own new wrinkle to the forming of the clay. After laying the coils in a rough approximation of the pot, the Hohokam woman shaped her pot with a paddle and anvil. The anvil was a small, convex piece of pottery or stone pressed against the inside of the pot, while a small flat stick was used to paddle the outside of the vessel to the desired contour. It was a delicate process, one requiring two steady hands, but the result was a finished product as fine as any made in the Southwest.

The Hohokam were also pithouse builders, but in design and construction they departed from the Mogollon formula. Most obviously, their homes were square or rectangular, and quite large; it was not unusual for a structure to be twenty to thirty feet in length on the long side. Probably most curious was the fact that they built an entire house inside the pit— they did not use the pit wall as a house wall. A ring of sticks and small posts would be sunk around the edge of the pit floor and laced with branches and brush. This framework was then packed and smeared with damp earth and clay, a technique known as wattle-and-daub, to form a solid barrier to the weather. The roof, sloping from central supports in a double pitch like a modern gambrel roof, was also covered with wattle-and-daub. The door was normally a sunken entry way on the long side of the structure, with the firepit located near the opening.

The Hohokam were desert people, living in a land where reliable water was the most elemental requirement for survival, and as a consequence they clustered their villages near the major rivers, the Gila and the Salt. They began to experiment with irrigation as early as A.D. 100, developing adequate and serviceable systems before 500, although it was nearly

700 before their skill and labor flourished into the extraordinary engineering projects that would rival modern efforts.

Working only with primitive digging sticks and baskets to move the earth and stone, the Hohokam carved their legacy into the desert on a baffling scale. One primary canal at Pueblo Grande, near Phoenix, was six feet deep and thirty feet wide; another measured ten feet deep and fifteen feet wide. From partial diversion dams on the Salt and Gila rivers, some of the canal networks reached as far as thirty miles inland to water the fields of the Hohokam. Lacking any sort of survey equipment, the Hohokam must have let the water show the way, filling a ditch and then cutting it further in the direction the water wanted to go. It was a haphazard approach, but there is no denying its effectiveness.

But it was not just the initial construction that speaks so eloquently for the Hohokam's determination; there was also the matter of maintaining such an extensive project. The Gila River was particularly unpredictable in its level of flow, necessitating constant adjustment to fill the system. Or a midsummer cloudburst could overtax an already full canal, washing out headgates and inundating everything downhill, cutting gullies across fields just ready to produce. The accomplishment bespeaks a high level of organization, for cooperation and division of labor within the community was absolutely essential to success.

Irrigation changed Hohokam life in other ways as well. Because the ditches required so much attention, the people became tied to the soil and ceased to wander at all. Large communities, like Snaketown, became almost totally dependent on agriculture, hunting only the rodents that naturally congregated around their fields. Irrigation became a self-perpetuating cycle: it begat a greater dependence and devotion to agriculture, which fostered larger sedentary communities, which in turn led to more irrigation. But because of the stability and security that came with irrigation, more time could be devoted to the arts and recreation—and here the Hohokam had some help.

As early as A.D. 500 the Hohokam began to demonstrate a marked Mexican influence in their lives.

They began to craft the small pyrite mirrors that the people of Meso-America had been making for centuries. Accomplished stone carvers in their own right, incising *metates* and stone bowls with designs and animistic bas-relief, the Hohokam began to carve stone into tiny, stylized human figurines—also a style from the south. Because they were fine craftsmen in stone, when the Hohokam abandoned the atlatl for the bow and arrow, they quickly became the Southwest's finest fashioners of arrow points. This might seem curious for a people who hunted rarely and then only rodents; one might expect the most assiduous hunters, the Mogollon, to make better projectiles. But the greater stone-carving skills of the Hohokam, plus possibly the greater leisure time afforded them by irrigation, gave the desert people this distinction.

Probably the most obvious example of the Hohokam's close ties to the south is manifested in the ball courts that began appearing after A.D. 500. The courts were oval structures of clay walls about six feet high, with an opening at each end large enough to admit a man. If the game as well as the court was derived from the south, it was probably very similar to the *pok-ta-pok* described by the earliest conquistadores of Mexico. The object was to get a small "rubber" ball (probably made from the gum of the guayu bush) through a hoop erected on one sidewall, without using the hands or feet. It has been suggested that these games may have had some religious function, although it may have been religion after the fashion of worshipers who gather on any given Sunday during the fall in our society's oval ball courts.

To secure their reputation as artisans, about A.D. 1000 the Hohokam developed a technique for etching animal and geometric motifs on seashells. The material was too brittle to carve, so the etching was most likely done with the highly acidic fermented juice of the saguaro cactus. The design was drawn on the shell with acid-resistant resins or pitch from desert plants, and the shell immersed in acid until enough shell was eaten away to give the design relief. Then the pitch was scraped off, leaving an ornament crafted by a technique that Europeans did not develop for another five hundred years.

The Hohokam would continue as a vital and sturdy culture until the time of the decline and reshuffling of all the great Southwest cultures about 1300. In the meantime, Hohokam influence would reach north to touch and shape the plateau, and with the rise of Anasazi would meld with it to create the satellite cultures of Salado and Sinagua. Despite the eventual disappearance of a distinc-tively Hohokam culture, the blood, spirit, and much of the cultural heritage of those people survives today among the Pima and Papago of Arizona.

The Mogollon and Hohokam, though emerging from a common root, developed separate and distinctive civilizations. They advanced sooner than the Anasazi of the plateau, gathering and creating a fund of knowledge and skills that would provide some of the building blocks in the rise of their backward neighbors to the north. At a time when the Mogollon and Hohokam had found the shape and direction of their lives, the Basket Maker Anasazi were still fumbling with the latchstring on the gate to a new life.

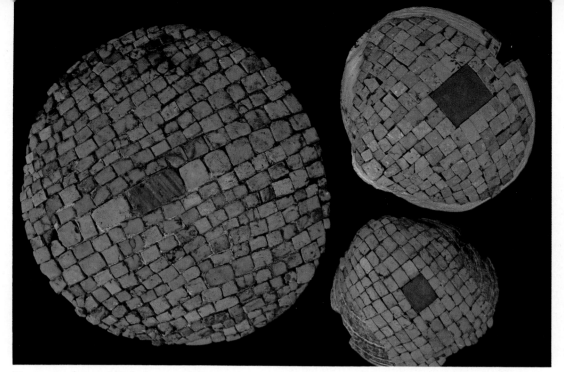

Turquoise frogs of Hohokam and Sinagua.

SINAGUA

The Sinagua were the people of the melting pot, a culture grown out of the meeting of Anasazi, Hohokam, and Mogollon in the land along the Little Colorado River to the north of modern Flagstaff, Arizona. The name Sinagua, Spanish for "without water," tells part of the story, for these people pursued survival as dry-land farmers, counting on the soil to absorb and hold enough water to nourish their crops through the growing cycle. Originally content as a scattered population of pithouse dwellers, the renaissance of Sinagua was brought on by the eruptions of Sunset Crater about A.D. 1000. Volcanic ash covered eight hundred square miles and, because of its moisture-retaining qualities, turned the region into a veritable garden, touching off a land rush.

Farmers of Anasazi, Hohokam, and Mogollon backgrounds streamed into the land immediately north of Sunset Crater, now known as Wupatki National Monument, bringing a variety of cultural baggage: village concepts, building techniques, arts, crafts, and religion. It was a peaceful collision, where skills and ideas were traded freely to form Sinagua. Hundreds of tiny villages sprang up, some with two- and three-story pueblos forming a centerpiece. But the pressure of so many farmers burned out the soil quickly, a loss which, combined with a sustained drought beginning in 1215, forced the Sinagua to leave the Wupatki region.

Increasing population pressure had led many Sinagua to depart even before the drought, and many filtered southward to the river-watered lands of Walnut Canyon and the Verde Valley. Here the irrigation skills that were part of the Hohokam contribution to the Sinagua cultural amalgam were put to use in farming the bottom lands along Beaver Creek at Montezuma Castle and along the Verde River at Tuzigoot. Here they raised once again the culture that built in the spirit of Anasazi and foreshadowed the blending of cultures that is modern Pueblo.

Overleaf: Sunrise on Wukoki ruin at Wupatki National Monument. The daily cycle of renewal that brought light and life to Sinagua reaffirmed the world's order.

Square House: How many hands and how many hours were required to create the city that rises in Wupatki? And in how many seasons will it all return to the earth?

Framed by the San Francisco Peaks, the ruins of Lomaki in Wupatki National Monument stand in silent testimony to man's dependence on the benificence of Nature: the instant the soil failed to produce, man departed.

Out of the living rock: A Sinagua ruin in
Walnut Creek Canyon National Monument.

A Sinagua pitcher and bowl acknowledge,
with their black-on-white design, close ties
to the Mesa Verde Anasazi.

Sleeping volcanoes and the skeleton of a yellow
pine in Sunset Crater National Monument are
silent reminders that all things have their season.

Grand Falls of the Little Colorado River during flood stage. In this land of extremes water is no exception—when it finally comes, it strikes with fury.

The Grand Canyon of the Colorado River from Mojave Point. Along the South Rim of the canyon lived for a brief time the Cohonina, a people whose close ties to the Anasazi taught them to build towers and homes of stone.

Montezuma Well in the Verde Valley, which was settled by Sinagua peoples from the Flagstaff-Wupatki region. Water from this great limestone sink filled the canals that irrigated their fields.

Montezuma Castle, a five-story pueblo that was home to probably fifty or more Sinagua, is tucked high into the limestone cliffs above Beaver Creek.

Moonrise over Tuzigoot: The Sinagua built a pueblo of over ninety rooms on this hilltop in the middle of the Verde Valley, farming the fertile alluvial bottoms around them.

Interior walls with metate and mano at Tuzigoot (an Apache word meaning "Crooked Water").

Gila polychrome pottery design.

SALADO

The Salado, prehistoric farmers of the ruggedly beautiful Tonto Basin country, drew their name from the Salt River (*Río Salado*), which flowed through the valley of their homeland. They were, like the Sinagua, the beneficiaries of the accumulated wisdom of their Anasazi neighbors to the north and the Hohokam gathered to the south along the low Salt and Gila rivers.

About A.D. 900, when Anasazi concepts first began to spread across the Southwest, the Salado were simple hunters and gatherers, but very quickly skills like pottery making began to filter in from the San Juan. Within two hundred years the Salado were farmers, living in small pueblos along the river valley, reflecting a recognizable version of the Anasazi parent culture. But the world of Hohokam was also visible, for the Salado developed as farmers who irrigated, diverting the waters of the Salt River onto their fields in a sophisticated network of canals.

Much of the Tonto Basin world of Salado was inundated by Roosevelt Dam, but the cliff dwellings nestled high in the mountains still remain to commemorate their ancient claim to this country—and to raise the question of why they chose to live four long, uphill miles from their fields. The need for the security of the rock must have been great.

The Salado were not wholly the recipients in the movement of cultures, however; they served as one of many avenues by which the skills of Anasazi reached down into the desert world of the Hohokam. The pueblo concept was adopted among the Hohokam, although it found less permanent expression in this land of adobe, as were polychrome pottery techniques, and the practice of burial without cremation. The Hohokam was an older, more static culture suddenly thrust in contact with the dynamism of the Anasazi—and the results are to be seen in the great desert pueblo of Casa Grande.

The three-color techniques that developed as Tonto polychrome were a result of the cultural mixing that typified both the Salado and the Sinagua.

Upper ruin at Tonto National Monument. Tucked away in steep canyon walls a thousand feet above, and four miles away from, their fields along the Salt River are the well-concealed and sturdy fortress pueblos that the Salado people built of unshaped quartzite and adobe.

Lower ruin at Tonto. This cliff dwelling of some twenty rooms was not built until about 1300; for two hundred years before, the Salado had been content with pueblos along the river plain—until some unnamed threat pushed them high into mountain citadels.

Water was the vital essence among the Hohokam desert dwellers; how well they controlled
its flow determined how well they lived—or even whether they survived.

The Hohokam pueblo of Casa Grande is built, not of stone, but of native caliche adobe.
To arrest its erosion, modern man has erected a structure of his own.

A Hohokam figure in a display at the Arizona
State Museum stands suspended in time
and imagination.

The frog, who followed water as nature dictated he should, was
an auspicious, even venerated creature to the irrigators of the desert
Southwest (here rendered in traditional Hohokam red-on-buff).

Small animistic clay figurines, a legacy to the Hohokam from
Mexican neighbors, were links to the natural world. Incense burners in shapes
of a man and a sheep probably served ceremonial functions.

Children at the Gate

The cultural explosion that reshaped the lives of the Mogollon and Hohokam in the first five hundred years of the Christian calendar hardly touched the Basket Maker Anasazi, who wandered among the valleys and mesas of the San Juan drainage high on the plateau. During a time when the people of the mountains and desert were settling down to a life of farms, houses, and pottery, the Basket Makers still enjoyed the rambling innocence of a grasshopper existence, drifting with the seasons, farming when the task did not prove too burdensome, and hunkering in caves or temporary shelters as the need arose.

But during the two hundred years after A.D. 500, real change entered the lives of these plateau country cousins, and they began to follow their more sophisticated neighbors from the south on a similar cultural path. The Basket Makers acquired the fundamentals of sedentary life, learning to build permanent houses and leaning more heavily on agriculture to supply their food. In the process they picked up other accomplishments of a higher level of civilization, most notably fired pottery and the bow and arrow. Permanent villages began to develop, alive with the mayhem of children, dogs, and domesticated turkeys.

Change did not come over the Basket Makers all at once, nor was the advance uniform across the entire plateau. It took fully two centuries to acquire and assimilate the tools of change, but this is a broad generalization at best, for the Basket Makers were not a homogeneous unit blessed with instant communication, so the process varied in time and intensity with each group on the plateau. Possibly because of a chance isolation from the mainstream of innovation, or maybe even an ingrained resistance to change, some pockets of population lagged far behind the general developments, dawdling in the backwater of a traditional Basket Maker lifeway. The story of Basket Maker development (and the whole saga of Anasazi, for that matter) is rife with exceptions and variations, but the change

97

The desert blooms: Poppies after a spring rain.

was generally widespread, and of sufficient moment to earn them a new name from the archaeologists: Modified Basket Makers.

Exactly where the plateau people picked up their new tricks cannot be known with any degree of certainty. It is apparent that they were an easygoing, gregarious folk who got on well with their neighbors and most strangers, a condition of personality that made trade with other regions of the Southwest a natural endeavor. Because of this trade, and some striking similarities of artifacts, it is most easily assumed that the Basket Makers learned much of what they did from the Mogollon and Hohokam. There is also the curious matter of a significant change in the shape of Basket Maker skulls that began to appear near the end of this period—a change that might lead the forthright and speculative to look for another, as yet invisible source of influence.

Whatever the impetus to change and innovation, the modification of the Basket Makers was a significant move forward in the lifeway that was Anasazi. It was the era that tripped the latch and swung wide the gate to the future for a developing and dynamic civilization on the plateau.

Basically, four qualities distinguished the Modified Basket Makers from their predecessors: a greatly increased dependence upon agriculture; the appearance of established communities of pithouses; the discovery of pottery; and the introduction of the bow and arrow. Each had a tremendous effect upon the lives of the developing Basket Makers, but the first two were so closely tied in a cause-and-effect relationship that they became almost one event.

When the Basket Makers first dabbled in agriculture as an adjunct to their hunting and gathering they began to discover that a man's labor invested in one place to plant, till, and harvest a crop, produced more food than that same labor turned to the task of chasing about the countryside looking for wild seeds and berries—and it also gave a surer return. Naturally, they began to devote more and more of their time to raising corn, and because they couldn't go wandering off when there were crops to be weeded, thinned, and protected from other hungry plateau critters, they were tied down through the spring and summer growth cycle.

Because they were stuck in one place, it was only natural to build houses with more permanence and greater comfort. Small villages, or irregular clusters of pithouses, arose where water was reliable and the vagaries of local climate conducive to growing corn. For the most part, those Modified Basket Makers who lived in caves moved down out of the cliffs to build their houses on open, flat ground. The reason they abandoned the caves is open to conjecture: perhaps they were fed up with the inconvenience of clambering up and down the cliffs; possibly the people from whom they learned built in the open, and the Basket Makers merely followed the example; or maybe they were escaping the cramped chill of the caves, where the sun warmed their nests for only a few hours each day.

Regardless of why they built in the open, the fact that they did leads to one undeniable conclusion: the Modified Basket Makers did not live in fear of attack by other peoples. A pithouse was a poor fortress, and scattered as they were in the open, these structures were even more vulnerable because they could be overwhelmed one at a time. With minor exception, to be detailed later, the Modified Basket Makers must have led a life uncomplicated by warfare.

It is possible that the Modified Basket Makers developed the pithouse themselves, independent of any outside influence, since it was a logical outgrowth of the slab-lined storage cists and thatch huts that were in evidence earlier in the San Juan region. As it evolved after A.D. 500, the pithouse was a circular hole, three to five feet deep and nine to twenty-five feet in diameter. The walls of the pit were often plastered with clay or lined with stone slabs, while the floor was usually left earthen, packed solid by the workmen's feet in the course of construction.

Faced with the problem of roofing the pit, a builder of typical Modified Basket Maker persuasion set off for the nearest pine stand with his stone axe. There he bludgeoned down eight trees about four to eight inches in diameter and trimmed off the excess foliage. Dragging the trees back to his pit, he cut four of them to the same length and sunk them in the floor to form the largest square possible within the circular pit. Into the forked tops of these posts, usually high enough for him to stand upright, he placed the other four large beams, forming a square framework. Next he laid slender poles about a foot apart, sloping from the edge of the pit up to the roof beams, and continued this latticework across the flat roof of the frame.

Then the builder went scavenging, scooping up brush, bark, and heavy grasses, and lashing it all to the skeletal roof to form a solid covering, leaving only a small smokehole near the center. Finally, he heaped several inches of earth over everything. From the outside it looked like a pile of dirt, but however humble its appearance, it proved an adequately weatherproof dwelling.

Originally, entrance was gained by a roofed tunnellike opening at one side, but as time passed the Modified Basket Makers apparently came to favor a ladder through the smokehole, for the side entrance was reduced in size until it was only a ventilator shaft. Inside the dwelling, between the interior opening of the ventilator and the firepit, a stone slab was erected to deflect the air coming in and reduce the velocity of drafts.

Beyond the firepit, in the center of the floor of the house, was the *sipapu*, a hole representing the opening through which man emerged onto the face of the earth. Apparently the pithouse of the Modified Basket Maker served as both home and ceremonial center. In some later houses, low walls of stone slab were erected on the floor, separating the pithouse into two distinct parts, possibly to prevent important ceremonial functions from being tainted by the humdrum of housework.

Toward the end of the period, about A.D. 700, pithouses began to become square or rectangular; during this same period the houses also began to come up out of the ground. But the basic concept of the pithouse, along with many of its features, would be preserved in the purely ceremonial structures —the kivas—of the Modified Basket Makers' descendants.

During the years when the Modified Basket Maker men were learning to build pithouses, their women were coming to grips with the arcane mysteries of pottery. Fired pottery did not originate among the Basket Makers; in fact, the Mogollon and Hohokam were fashioning it hundreds of years before the first homegrown pots appeared on the plateau. Curiously, though, it seems that the Basket Makers were not the beneficiaries of all their southern neighbors' cumulative wisdom, for plateau pottery crumbled its way through a period of experimental gropings, indicating that while they may have gotten the idea from someone else, they certainly did not pick up the techniques as well.

The idea probably reached the Basket Makers when one of their men ranged far to the south on a trading expedition and saw—perhaps bartered for—a pot in a Mogollon or Hohokam village. Whatever the origin of the concept, Basket Maker women turned to the task with enthusiasm—but initially met with less than unqualified success.

They tried sun-drying plain clay pots, which got soggy and washed away when filled with water. They experimented with firing plain clay, but it cracked and fell to powder. They dabbled with bark and grass mixed into the clay, which held the pot together nicely during firing but had a nasty habit of developing leaks over open fires when the grass burned all the way through the pot. Finally, they found that mixing sand and other materials with the clay, as a temper before shaping and firing, yielded satisfactory results.

In time the Modified Basket Makers introduced a new wrinkle into the process that dramatically distinguished their pottery from Mogollon and Hohokam: they used a radically different method to fire their wares. Pottery of the Mogollon and Hohokam was predominantly buff, yellow, and red, due in large measure to firing in an oxidizing (oxygen-rich) atmosphere. Modified Basket Maker pottery, on the other hand, ran to dull gray, the result of firing in an oxygen-free atmosphere.

Since they did not have kilns, which could be regulated to exclude oxygen, the Modified Basket Makers had to bake their pottery in the middle of a small, flaming pyre of dry wood and brush. A rapidly burning fire, as opposed to the slow coals of the Mogollon and Hohokam, would itself consume all of the available oxygen, leaving the pot to bake in the oxygen-free center of the fire. Considering the critical nature of firing in the process, it is unlikely that the plateau people would have developed their own technique if they had had one to emulate.

For the most part, Modified Basket Maker pottery was a plain, dull gray with a rough and often uneven exterior. While it wasn't fancy, it was serviceable; and to a people keenly interested in turning out a new and useful tool in large numbers, serviceability was more important than aesthetics. The pots were mostly squat, globular shapes, formed by using the coil-and-scrape technique prevalent among the Mogollon. Some were decorated, and for designs the Modified Basket Makers mostly imitated the patterns they had developed in their baskets, using parallel lines, triangles, dots, and a few crude life forms of familiar animals. The designs were painted with vegetable colors that carbonized and turned black with the firing, rendering the first of the black-on-gray (and later black-on-

white) ornamentation that would typify the pottery of the San Juan.

Because of their incessant trading activities, the Basket Makers acquired some finely crafted and intricately decorated red pots from the Mogollon or Hohokam early in their pottery careers. Baffled by the color, but impressed with its appearance, the women of the plateau squandered many an afternoon trying to re-create it. Their determination was rewarded only with frustration, for no matter what they tried, the pot invariably came out of their reducing fire either black or gray. But they were not to be denied, and in desperation they concocted a red slip of vegetable dyes and applied it *after* firing. It didn't seem to matter that the effect was impermanent and not very attractive; at least it was red.

The discovery of pottery, besides making life easier, also opened up new avenues in agriculture. It is very likely that the Modified Basket Makers knew about beans before they knew about pottery, but without pots the bean was virtually useless. Imagine, if you will, an early Basket Maker wife and mother on the Mesa Verde faced with the prospect of converting this new pebble-sized and pebble-hard bounty from her husband's garden into something edible. She tried mashing the beans into meal, but that was not very satisfactory, so she decided to cook them until they got soft. The altitude was about 7,000 feet, where water boils at a very low temperature, and anything boiled can take a very long time to cook. After three hours of juggling hot rocks into a leaky basket of water and beans, and still finding them hard enough to chip an incisor, it is likely that she gave her man some direct and pungent advice on what not to plant next year.

Pottery changed all that, for now she could put her pot close to the coals of the cook fire and leave it to bubble all day long, with no attention from her save an occasional stir and the addition of a little water now and again. Although they never reached the stature of corn in the Southwest diet, beans were a rich new source of protein and a reassuring hedge against the bet every man made on the success of the annual corn crop.

Although the Modified Basket Makers were abandoning the old wandering lifeway for the security and prosperity of sedentary agriculture, they still continued to be hunters on an enthusiastic scale. The atlatl spear had been the primary weapon throughout much of the period, but shortly before A.D. 700 the bow and arrow began to appear. Its adoption wrought no great changes in the hunting habits of the Basket Makers, but it unquestionably increased their effectiveness, which in turn contributed to the settled quality of their lives by allowing them to spend more time at home.

Since both the Mogollon and Hohokam to the south were using the bow and arrow long before the Anasazi, it is easy to assume that the idea found its way to the plateau by a natural process of diffusion. Unfortunately, there are no guarantees that this was the case. It is known that Basket Makers living in Canyon de Chelly had come in contact with someone carrying a bow before A.D. 650, because a woman was killed with an arrow, but whether it was the result of a domestic squabble or a raid by outsiders will never be known.

The Modified Basket Makers continued to hunt not only to eat but to gather the raw materials for winter clothes as well. They still relied heavily on the rabbit for cloaks their ancestors had taught them to fashion, but during this era of change they began adding turkey-feather mantles to their wardrobe. The construction was much the same as that used to make the fur robes; the feathers were split along the quill and wrapped around long strands of twine to make feather ropes, which in turn were laced together side-by-side with more twine. Quite often both feather and fur ropes were combined into a single warm winter cloak.

The curious thing is that the Anasazi apparently did not get their turkey feathers by hunting. Sometime during this period the Modified Basket Makers had managed to domesticate the turkey, and it was from these flocks that the feathers came. It also seems that they did not eat the birds, but kept them just for the plumage. The Anasazi had also domesticated the dog—possibly even before they were first recognizable as Basket Makers —but unlike the Plains Indians, who considered roast canine a delicacy, the Anasazi did not eat their dogs either. Such a circumstance speaks well for their success as farmers and hunters, or maybe just for their regard for their pets.

The domestication of turkeys presents a puzzle, though, because as any farm boy who ever straw-bossed a barnyard knows, turkeys are the foulest-tempered, dumbest, most contrary and exasperating critters man has ever sought to tame. Wild turkeys are wily and man-shy, but once domesticated they rapidly become insufferably arrogant. The problems the turkey must have generated for the Modified Basket Makers might best be illustrated by an incident that occurred at Mesa Verde not too many years ago.

The staff at the national park there reintroduced turkeys to the area with the hope that the birds would add a little of the old flavor to the ruins. Before long they had added a lot more than anyone bargained for—stalking the roads and tying up traffic, raiding the gardens of staff residents, moving onto porches at the visitor center during inclement weather and refusing to leave. They stole food, crowded inside houses when doors were left ajar, and worst of all, they defecated on everything. Turkeys are copious producers of waste, and soon walkways, ruins, clothes hung out to dry, little children, and visitors were festooned.

The rangers then undertook to drive the birds away, to frighten them back into a wild state. Shots fired overhead rattled the turkeys momentarily, but they quickly adjusted to the noise. Firecrackers and rocks thrown at them had no further effect (except when one turkey tasted a cherry bomb just before it exploded). The birds simply would not be driven away by fear.

Man finally prevailed, and the turkey hordes were successfully banished from the housing areas of Mesa Verde, but without modern ploys the problem must have been monumental for the Anasazi. It has been suggested that the Anasazi did not actually domesticate the turkey—the birds just moved in, and the only way to control them was to have the children herd them around. But that explanation fails to take into account the recently acquired bow and arrow, which would have solved the free-loading turkey problem in short order. Whatever its origin, the turkey was there to stay, and the Anasazi somehow managed to learn to live with it.

The Modified Basket Maker Anasazi continued to fashion baskets after the discovery of pottery, although storage bags and waterproof vessels declined as pots began to do the job better. The baskets that were made became even more elaborate, exhibiting a careful attention to intricacies of decoration worked in red and black. No longer the universal tool, the basket was moving into the realm of art.

Sandals also improved during this period, especially the finer, dress-up footwear. A distinctive crescent-toed shape began to develop, in which the old square front was replaced by one with a concave curve at the toe, probably the result of tying the warp strands to a hoop rather than a straight bar while weaving. The sandal was made in two layers, a finely woven top laced with colored strands in a decorative design, and a bottom layer done in a coarse, wide pattern with deep relief to give good traction.

Until the end of the Modified Basket Maker era (about A.D. 700) the Anasazi women also clung to a tradition of making cradleboards that dated back to the earliest Basket Makers. The cradleboard, to which the Anasazi infant was strapped for much of his first year, was a soft, flexible affair fashioned by weaving reeds and yucca twine across a wooden hoop, and padded with mulched bark or fur. This device allowed the mother to carry or tend her child with a minimum of distraction.

But the Anasazi infant was about to lose his soft cradleboard, as would all those who followed him, for his people were caught up in the dynamics of change, and the cradle was only part of the story. The Modified Basket Makers had brought change to their own lives and the lives of their children for generations to come, but it was not to stop there. For the lifeway that was Anasazi, it was only the beginning.

Anasazi corrugated earthenware jars.

CANYONS AND MESAS

The culture we call Anasazi was a lifeway created out of the earth, molded and shaped by the land and its elemental forces. It was a world created by people moving up the central path of survival and fulfillment, channeled by the twin guideposts of what they needed and what the land had to offer. They did not make the land over in their own image, but accommodated their lives to its dictates—emerging in the end with a life in balance with nature, a most efficient response to the challenge of the environment.

It was a culture adjusted to the semiarid desert and plateau country of the Southwest; it could—and did—spring up in often small pockets of population where water was even marginally sufficient for survival. Anasazi civilization reached northwest from the Four Corners into the plateau country around the confluence of the Colorado and Green rivers, in what today is Canyonlands National Park. Isolated ruins are scattered all across south-eastern and southcentral Utah, testimony in stone to the vitality and adaptability of the culture. The Anasazi way found a foothold in the barren expanses of Monument Valley, among the monoliths sculpted by shadow play with both earth and sky. Close by Four Corners the villages of Hovenweep rose up to guard the tiny canyons that etch fine lines across the high rolling land. Here the Anasazi built carefully, with a pride and skill that endures in some of the finest freestanding ruins extant.

Southwest of Four Corners, between the awesome and inspiring cliffs that frame Canyon de Chelly, the pageant of Anasazi evolved through all the stages of its growth, from Basket Maker to the culminant Classic Pueblo—of which evidence remains today. The name is an English corruption of a Spanish corruption word *Tsegi*—"rock canyon" in Navajo, which language has no relation to the Anasazi. They probably called it simply home.

Sunrise in Monument Valley reflects the return of the earth to life with each morning's dawn.

Hidden away from the blaze of the midday sun, like homes of all the other creatures of the desert, a sandstone cliff dwelling in Mystery Valley stands as epitaph to the hopes of the Anasazi who passed this way.

An elemental land, sculpted by wind and water, marks the river's ageless course through Canyon de Chelly; Nature's grand artistry in carving cathedral cliffs and monumental arches humbles man and yet fills his spirit in one deft stroke. But to the Anasazi it was probably more significant that the Rio de Chelly had also laid down a fertile bed of soil on which to raise a civilization.

The white plaster wall that gave White House its name flares bright as the ruin stares out on the last light of day in Canyon de Chelly.

Tower ruin in Horse Canyon, Canyonlands National Park, stands beyond reach of the danger that pushed its people here, but time and a myriad of pressures have eroded even this sanctuary.

The water that long ago carved the sandstone caves where the Anasazi built often continues to flow, running down in a gentle fountain near the rear of the cave.

A cave painting, now known as the All-American Man, in Salt Creek Canyon, Utah. One can only wonder what visions of prophecy must have been conjured in the quiet of the kiva.

Onto the Rock

During their brief tenure as guardians of the lifeway that was Anasazi, the Basket Makers had brought shape and direction to life on the plateau. The world of the Ancient Ones on the flat tableland of Mesa Verde, the narrow valley of Chaco Canyon, the tangled canyons of Kayenta to the west, and the cathedral cliffs of Canyon de Chelly, was a tableau of successful agricultural villages cast in high relief against a grudgingly semiarid terrain. In scores of other spots where water and soil offered the raw materials of farming and the seasons laid down harmonious ambient themes on the landscape, the Basket Makers had grappled with discovery and pointed the way to the future.

The second great era of Anasazi, which began about A.D. 700, is known as the Pueblo horizon. The era draws its name from the Spanish word meaning "village," which the conquistadores applied to the Indian communities as early as the sixteenth century. While the term has not lost its original meaning, in the Southwest it has also come to be used to define the large, multiroomed adobe and stone communal dwellings occupied by the native residents of the region—which are not to be confused with the myriad of other large, multiroomed adobe and stone communal dwellings, emblazoned with neon and offers of free continental breakfasts, that now dot the Southwest in even greater abundance.

The early phase of this new era, which has generally become known as Developmental Pueblo, spanned three and a half centuries or more, to the latter half of the eleventh century. During the Developmental Pueblo phase the Anasazi began the tradition of stone masonry, a skill that left the most enduring monuments to their passing. They brought their homes up out of the earth and at the same time pushed their ceremonial centers—kivas—deeper into it.

It was a time of tremendous population growth on the plateau, and the developments of Anasazi culture began spreading east to the upper reaches of the Rio Grande drainage basin, south to the land of the Mogollon and

The castlelike dwellings at Hovenweep were probably built by displaced Anasazi from Mesa Verde.

Hohokam, and west and north to peripheral Desert Culture peoples along the great Colorado River system.

It was a time of great change for the Anasazi, a condition which was rapidly becoming a way of life for these culturally dynamic people. In the past they had borrowed profusely from everyone they had met, but they were embarking on a period of development and innovation that would make them the lenders. And almost as if to commemorate the dawn of a new era, the physical appearance of the Anasazi changed dramatically.

When twentieth-century archaeologists first began to unravel the mystery of the Anasazi, they discovered that the Basket Makers were a people of long, narrow heads (dolichocephalic), while the later Pueblo people had a head that was much broader (brachycephalic). Initially it was assumed that they were two entirely different groups of people, that a greatly advanced group of broadheaded newcomers had arrived in the Four Corners area and supplanted the narrowheaded and relatively backward Basket Makers. Such an invasion would account for the extraordinary cultural advances made about this time: the bow and arrow, the distinctive pottery, and the stone masonry that was unique in the Southwest.

Further investigation and a lot of hard digging revealed, however, that there was no great influx of broad-headed mystery people from nobody-knew-where, but rather that the Basket Makers had simply adopted a practice of cranial deformation. They had suddenly taken to flattening the backs of their children's heads by strapping the new infants to hard, rigid cradleboards. They completely abandoned the flexible, padded cradleboard that had been an unswerving tradition through centuries marked by change in other respects and substituted a flat, unpadded board. The result on the malleable skull of a baby was predictable; the back of the head

flattened and the sides bulged, resulting in a person who appeared broad-headed for the rest of his days.

It has commonly been the practice to explain away this curious trend as merely a change in fashion, much as modes of hair, figure, and dress change today. It is a pleasing analysis that is easy on the sensibilities, but like the "ceremonial objects" catch-all that is used to explain artifacts with no apparent practical utility, the question might better be left open-ended.

The adoption of the rigid cradleboard could possibly have an extraordinary significance, especially when it is noted that there were some genuinely broad-headed people living in the eastern reaches of the San Juan drainage about this time. They were very few, certainly not enough to alter the racial stock of the Anasazi even if they were prolific breeders, but there may have been enough of these people to set the standard by which the late Basket Makers measured themselves.

Suppose, for a moment, that the broadheads were a truly advanced people—stonemasons, archers, and artisans in pottery and jewelry of a high order—who wandered onto the plateau late in the seventh century. Harold Gladwin, a scholar who toiled industriously amid the shards of Southwest prehistory armed with a maverick imagination, argued felicitously in favor of a migrating Mexican or Central American group who made their way up the west coast of Mexico and across the Southwest, spreading the gospel of fired pottery and the accoutrements of civilization. Maybe there was no migration of messianic peoples, but a few stray broad-heads came from somewhere, with the possibility that they carried new ideas.

Imagine the impact of such a meeting on the Anasazi. Here were a people of considerable accomplishments, with answers for questions no one on the plateau had even asked. They were brilliant, perhaps leaders in the community by virtue of their knowledge, and therefore much to be imitated. A mother, seeking the best for her child, might go to any lengths to pattern her progeny after the new mental giants—even to the shape of the head. Perhaps, then, the rigid cradleboard appeared simply as a tool for achieving new status among the Anasazi, and the broad head remained as a standard of intelligence and accomplishment.

Far-fetched? No more so, certainly, than mashing a child's head out of shape on the off chance that it might look charming. But whatever the details might be, while it might be plausible that cranial deformation was an attempt to imitate some advanced broad-headed people, it is just as likely that it was not. Hopefully the Anasazi themselves knew why they did it.

This era called Developmental Pueblo is aptly named, for it was during these years, from A.D. 700 to 1050 or 1100, that the Anasazi experimented with progressively more sophisticated and time-consuming building techniques, ultimately evolving the fine masonry that characterized the classic, and final, era. The development was not uniform or universal; in some areas, Chaco Canyon most notably, great structures boasting hundreds of rooms of finely fitted masonry were completed by A.D. 950, while builders farther to the west had barely transcended wattle-and-daub by 1100. Any confident generalities about when or how Anasazi building methods evolved can be whittled down to trembling suppositions by the nagging inconsistency of a hundred exceptions, but a basic outline of events can be cast without doing too much violence to that phantom called Truth.

Under the hand of the early Pueblo Anasazi, the pithouse of the Modified Basket Makers evolved in two directions: it climbed up out of its shallow hole to stand on the surface as a house, and it burrowed deeper as a kiva, carrying many pithouse features with it and becoming more formalized in the process. Almost without exception the Developmental Pueblo completed the trend begun by the Modified Basket Makers and brought their homes and villages out onto the mesas and river valleys, spurning the cliffs and caves entirely.

Very early in this period, especially at the more dynamic cultural centers in Chaco Canyon, Mesa Verde, and Kayenta, the Anasazi began living communally, gradually abandoning individual pithouses in favor of slightly curved rows of contiguous rooms. The earlier surface structures may have been storage rooms built behind the inhabited pithouses, but the Anasazi soon found the style to their liking and adapted it to dwellings. In these flat-roofed, single-story affairs, each room served to house an entire family, and although the style was probably not conceived as a labor-saving device, it did allow a man to use a wall of his neighbor's house for one wall of his own.

Typically the dwellings faced the inside of the curve, and in most instances deep pit-houses, and later formalized kivas, were arranged in front of the long house to meet the group's ceremonial needs. In the instance of Mesa Verde, the pattern became formalized at a very early date, and for reasons not thoroughly understood, all across the mesa the small pueblos were arranged on a northwest-to-southeast orientation. The houses stood on the northwest edge of a site facing southeast, with the kivas in front of them, while further to the southeast was the trash dump. The institutional trinity of home, church, and garbage common to all Anasazi was occasionally repeated with this same directional orientation in other areas of the Four Corners region.

The earliest of the multiroom "unit" houses clung tenaciously to the old ways, with the floor sunken as much as a foot into the ground. The walls, however, already displayed a new departure—construction by a method now called jacal. Slender posts were set in the ground, usually only a few inches apart, and the space between them was packed with

The earliest Anasazi cities, like those of their Pueblo Indian descendants, were built on open mesas.

adobe. The job probably proceeded by stages; packing the wet adobe gradually higher until it threatened to collapse of its own weight, allowing it to be baked by the sun, and then raising the wall higher still. Around the base of the house, stone slabs were placed against the wall and mortared into place with adobe. While their utility is suspect, these slabs mark the beginning of exterior stone masonry.

The roofs were laid down after the pattern developed by the Basket Makers, a method that remained substantially unchanged through the end of Anasazi culture. Between the stout side beams at the top of the walls were placed slender cross poles, with brush and small branches laid in a tight layer across them. Then a layer of mud or earth several inches thick was spread over the brush work, leaving an opening as a smoke hole near the center. The roof had to be sturdily built, because the flat housetops were a favorite work area of Anasazi women.

The methods employed to raise the walls of the unit houses changed gradually under the hands and imaginations of succeeding generations. The jacal technique was modified by dispensing with the stone slabs at the base of the wall, placing the posts a foot or more apart, and packing the spaces with adobe that had small stones mixed through it.

The first true masonry appeared when the Anasazi quit using the posts as a framework and built their walls using only stone and adobe. Larger rocks, which the builders made no attempt to shape, were laid irregularly and packed solidly with adobe. The walls were crude stonework, and usually 50 percent adobe at that, but if they were not aesthetically pleasing, at least they were sturdy.

Late in the Developmental Pueblo era the Anasazi began to show the genius for stonework that would distinguish their culture from all others. The amount of adobe mortar began to diminish, because the rock became more carefully fitted. While this seems a logical evolution, it was nonetheless a big step, for the sandstone building blocks were chipped to size and shape with stone tools only slightly harder than sandstone. The work was slow, and tools wore out quickly, forcing a man to suspend building altogether while he fashioned new tools.

The first shaping was applied only to the bearing surfaces, marrying the sandstone along even joints and arranging regular rows and layers of rockwork. The mortar took on a secondary importance, structurally and visually, as the essential stability of the masonry relied more on careful fitting and stacking. Eventually the builders began shaping the visible facing sides of the building blocks, too, until the walls showed a smooth and even facade.

As the masonry technique was refined, the size and complexity of the buildings increased. Pueblos two stories high were built, and the number of storage and living rooms sometimes reached thirty or more in a single contiguous building. Although there were notable exceptions, most of the villages remained somewhat small during this time. Under the pressure of tremendous population growth the Anasazi were spreading out, building new towns and moving in on less dynamic neighbors, rather than herding together in the great cities that typified the later, classic period.

The evolutionary development that beset housebuilding was also reflected in the kivas. While he brought his houses to the surface, the Anasazi kept his religion underground, keeping with it virtually all of the floor features that had characterized the late Basket Maker pithouse. At first, the subterranean ceremonial cells that burrowed in front of the pueblos were nothing more than deep pithouses, plastered on the inside with smooth caliche adobe. In time, a bench running all the way around was hewed out of the earth, and the roof-support posts rose from it instead of from the floor. The posts were eventually replaced by stone pilasters, on which the roof beams rested.

The Anasazi brought their stone craftsmanship to the kiva, lining all the walls, and occasionally the floor, with closely fitted and carefully shaped sandstone. The archetypal clan kiva was usually not more than twenty-five feet in diameter. At one side a ventilator shaft ran straight down from outside the kiva, turning at a right angle to emerge at floor level inside the structure. A few feet in front of the ventilator opening stood a low stone slab or wall which served as a deflector to disperse the draft. Beyond the deflector was the firepit, and beyond it in a straight line, at the center of the floor, was the sipapu, the symbolic entryway of man into the world.

The stone-lined bench that circled the floor offered a seating surface normally two or three feet high and more than a foot deep. From the bench rose six to eight masonry pilasters on which rested the primary roof beams. The flat roof at ground level had a smoke hole in the center, which also served as the entrance by means of a ladder.

The function of the kiva, and its role in Pueblo Anasazi life, cannot be known for certain, but inferences drawn from modern Pueblo Indian society may provide a reliable outline, because these people may very well be the direct cultural descendants of the Anasazi. If that is the case, the kiva was the center of Anasazi ceremonial life, where religious activities were carried out by the men of the village. Each kiva was the province of a single society, and any village might have several societies—each different, each important for a particular skill at influencing the supernatural, but all dedicated to the continuing good fortune of the entire village.

The kiva also served as a clubhouse for the men of its society, an important function considering a man's peculiar position in the community. The Anasazi were matrilineal, tracing their ancestry through mothers, and for this reason women wielded considerable influence in temporal affairs. The home of a couple was owned by the wife, and important decisions were made by her family, not her husband's. A young boy growing up on the plateau lived in his mother's house and was taught the ways of manhood largely by her brothers and other male relatives. As he turned the corner into adolescence, he was inducted into a kiva society, usually one closely affiliated with the male members of his mother's family. When he married, he moved into his wife's house—and into the domain of his mother-in-law. In any domestic squabbles he was at a distinct numerical disadvantage, blood being thicker than the bonds of matrimony; if the discord ran too deep, his wife could throw him out entirely.

His only refuge was the kiva, where women were absolutely forbidden, except as participants in certain ceremonies. He could retreat there with other disgruntled husbands and the young unmarried men to talk, work, or plot a return to marital harmony. It was his own place, where he was always a person of some stature. Of course, if the kiva didn't satisfy him, he could always go meddle in the affairs of his sister's family. Men were not second-class citizens throughout Anasazi society —just in their own homes.

The Developmental Pueblo people did not ignore their other crafts during this era of architectural advance. Pottery was distinguished by greater skill in manufacture and decoration, and a new style was developed, differentiating cooking ware from storage and serving vessels. Early in the period the Anasazi women began to leave the top coils on their plain gray cooking jars unsmoothed. The coils were not usually in the form of a single continuous band climbing on top of itself, but rather as separate, complete loops, and with another distinct coil laid above it. By late in Developmental Pueblo times, this penchant for not smoothing the neck of the vessel had spread to the entire pot. Corrugated culinary ware became common and required nothing more of the potter than that she not smooth the dimpled surface that was created as she pinched the coils of clay together.

Several explanations for this new style are possible. The least likely is that Anasazi women had grown lazy and did not want to

A corrugated surface distinguished cookware from other Developmental Pueblo pottery.

The bold, black-on-white geometric designs that characterized Anasazi pottery evolved early.

Archaeologists find it hard to date petroglyphs, but these in Dinosaur National Monument, Utah, were probably the work of the Fremont people, who lived northwest of the Anasazi.

bother scraping the surface smooth. In fact, the neatly corrugated vessels may have required more care to make than a coiled pot, roughly pinched and smoothed for painting. More probably the women had discovered that this was the only kind of decoration that was not obliterated by the soot and smoke of the cooking fire. Another dividend from the corrugated pots, which they probably did not anticipate but may have perceived later, is the thermal efficiency of the design. A pot corrugated on the outside and smooth on the inside conducts more heat faster than one that is smooth on both sides.

In their decorated pottery the Anasazi continued the tradition of black-on-white, raising the craft to new levels of beauty. The most distinctive change came in the realm of color, as the Developmental Pueblo women turned increasingly to the use of slips to achieve a bright white background for their black designs. The slips were a fine, light clay, thinned with water to a very liquid consistency and carefully applied to the pot before firing. To the east, in the vicinity of Chaco Canyon, the black paints were made from minerals, while those to the west were predominantly vegetable based. Another regional distinction, not related to the paints, can be also seen: eastern pots showed designs in sharp relief against the background, because the designs were applied after polishing and before firing the pot; in the west, where designs were applied before polishing and firing, the edges of the black designs faded somewhat into the white, giving a softer, less precise look to the pottery.

The skill and patience brought to basket-making declined drastically toward the end of Developmental Pueblo times, a natural casualty of the greater interest in pottery. The craftsmanship in sandal-making also regressed as the Anasazi lost the keen sense for weaving grasses. Serviceable footwear was in abundance, and the crescent-toe configuration was replaced by a notch design on one side of an otherwise round toe; but the artistry of decoration was waning.

Another new dimension was added to their lives when cotton was introduced to the Anasazi. The plant was grown by the Hohokam at an earlier date, but it is difficult to know how or when the Developmental Pueblo learned of it. Although they did have some cotton cloth, it is unclear whether they traded for it, or grew and wove it themselves. Cotton cloth is simply too perishable an item to leave much record of its passage.

During the era of Developmental Pueblo the Anasazi came into their own, creating a culture that was distinctive, maybe even transcendent. Anasazi settlements reached across the entire plateau, even planting the seeds of their future in tiny villages on the northern Rio Grande. The vitality of their lifeway, and the innovations that were its result, spread south to influence and alter the culture of a static, even dying Mogollon. They had begun the march that would lead them to the south and west, sharing their knowledge with the Hohokam and creating new cultures by that cross-fertilization.

Whatever the reasons for it, the Anasazi were a changed people. They had become builders of a solid permanence, the innovators rather than the imitators in the Southwest scheme. They had worked hard to create the tools and institutions of a stable and ordered world, which they would refine and enjoy in a final florescence.

Black-on-white design from Aztec National Monument.

CHACO CANYON

First to bloom and first to perish, Chaco Canyon was the most obvious realization of the Anasazi penchant for urban living. In this narrow canyon braced by high bluffs and gashed down the center by Chaco Wash, the Anasazi built twelve great pueblo cities, tied together by a network of wide and defined trails. Smaller groups of dwellings rose on the mesas immediately above the canyon and along the foot of the cliffs—sufficient in all to house the population of seven thousand that occupied the canyon during the boom years late in the eleventh century.

Here where a single pueblo might bring a thousand people together in a three-tiered sandstone warren, the sense of community was felt daily—and apparently enjoyed. From the rooftops and plazas, where most of the labor of everyday life was done, the entire village was visible, making everyone a witness to almost every secular event in the community and tying them all together in the web of shared experience.

The concentration of population in Chaco Canyon was the direct consequence of the Chacoans' high level of efficiency in agriculture, for the population could not grow without a surplus of food and the arable land in the vicinity was far from infinite. To feed seven thousand people on the available land, the villagers must have harvested on a yield-per-acre ratio that rivals modern returns—and they did so apparently without fighting over growing rights on the more productive land.

The world of Chaco Canyon was mirrored in the massive village of Aztec Ruins far to the north. A great horseshoe-shaped pueblo of five hundred rooms, Aztec was built under the strong influence of Chacoans about A.D. 1100 and then abandoned—to be reoccupied by peoples of a definite Mesa Verde background. The cycle was completed when the villagers of Aztec joined the general Anasazi exodus from familiar haunts late in the thirteenth century, leaving their home to time and the elements.

Their perishable roofs of timber and earth long since destroyed by the desert elements,
the clan kivas of Pueblo Bonito spread out across the plaza. Although these were built above
ground level, Chacoans achieved a subterranean effect by filling in the spaces between.

The urban instincts of the Chacoans are revealed even in the much decayed pueblo of
Chettro Kettle. Its labyrinth of rooms, sometimes stacked three stories high, hints
rather broadly at the occupants' peaceful, tolerant nature—an essential ingredient
in the maintenance of amicable relations with one's neighbors.

*At the core of Anasazi life was man's relationship
to the powers that brought order to Nature, hence
the importance of the kiva. But these people were
also gregarious and communal—hence the great kiva,
as here at Pueblo Bonito.*

*Many of the pottery techniques practiced in
Chaco Canyon reflected a strong influence of Mesa Verde
traditions, as in the case of this black-on-white olla.*

Pueblo Bonito represents life as the Anasazi preferred it—a close-quartered city on an open plain. Until they were driven to the safety of the cliffs, most of their cities were built this way.

In a world where religion and the course of everyday events were inseparable, ceremonial kivas were as basic to life as rooms for sleeping or cooking— and often seem to modern eyes nearly as numerous.

Pueblo del Arroyo, another large village less than half a mile from Bonito. For all
the outward similarities to modern apartment and urban life, Chacoans did not suffer
the feelings of anonymity that prevail today. A sense of community, bolstered by blood
ties, naturally arose because every individual was essential to the village's survival.

Despite past grandeur, the spectre of defeat and loneliness lies heavy on Chaco.

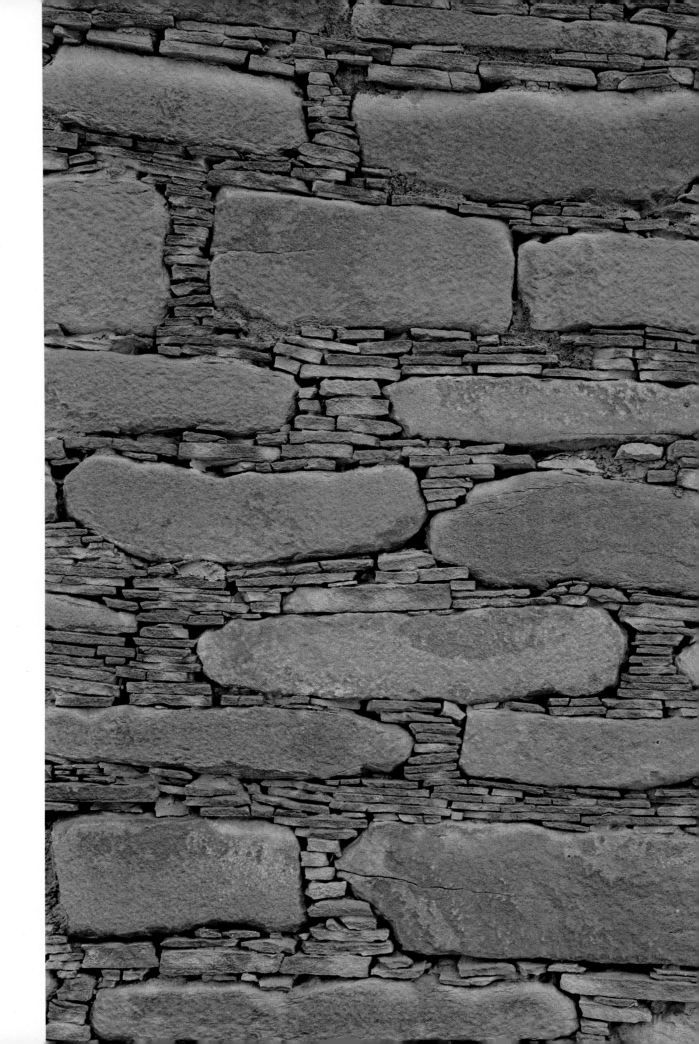

Above: The largest of the great kivas in Chaco Canyon, Casa Rinconada.
Left: Although originally hidden behind a smooth plaster of adobe, the counterpoint of
delicacy and mass renders exposed Chaco walls the most pleasing of any built by the Anasazi.
Curiously, this attractive facade masks still another, inner wall of rubble.

Another of the dozen or so large cities that string down the narrow valley, Kin Kletso
added its bulk to the urban sprawl of Chaco Canyon. In a bold departure from local
form, however, the stonework was uniformly more massive, reminiscent of Mesa Verde.

Doorways: Aztec National Monument.

*Interior of the reconstructed great kiva at Aztec
National Monument. Similar in purpose to those
of Chaco, the great kiva met ceremonial needs that
transcended the scope of the clan kivas.*   135

In the utility and artistry of Chaco pottery one sees the fine balance of aesthetic sensitivity and pragmatic response to challenge that permeated its makers' lives.

Sons of Light

From the time the earliest Basket Maker planted a kernel of corn in the virgin soil of the Four Corners region and discovered a partial alternative to the migratory habits of his forebears, the Anasazi had been toiling toward a new way of living. Vigorous, inquisitive, and adaptable, they had created an intricate culture in a land that even today resists the inroads of man. In less than a thousand years, a distinctive civilization had been forged out of hard work, ingenuity, and a few timely hints from distant neighbors.

Their efforts culminated in the era we know as Great, or Classic, Pueblo, and for two hundred years, roughly from A.D. 1100 to 1300, the Anasazi enjoyed the full measure of their fathers' progress. It was a time marked by the most impressive and enduring buildings and the finest pottery. They were the beneficiaries of countless generations' hard-won experience and tools for farming and hunting; society was orderly, with well-defined responsibilities and rewards that provided an intangible security with self; they were freed from the urgency of

scraping together the bare necessities of survival; and they had learned to specialize, each doing what he did best and trading his surplus for what else he needed. For the Anasazi of Classic Pueblo times, life was full and good. Of all the Southwest cultures, the Anasazi were the most fortunate—the chosen people, the children of light.

During these years they began congregating to form much larger villages, building the great multistoried apartment dwellings for which they are best remembered. Initially, the movement into these fortresslike warrens was probably the result more of desire than of need, for if fear were the motive, there would have been little time for the careful craftsmanship that the buildings exhibit. Later in the period defense may have become a more compelling factor, but in the beginning the Anasazi built leisurely and deliberately.

The creation of these cities was an enormous project, indicating a high level of organization within the community. Because there is no evidence of a distinct ruling class, cooperation must have been the key to success. The Anasazi had apparently learned to sacrifice part of their individual labor and freedom of choice for the good of the entire community, to profit indirectly from the improved condition of society as a whole. The unspoken corollary here, of course, is increased regimentation, but judging from their precise observance of formal custom in art and religion, this was nothing alien or repugnant to the Anasazi.

The three great cultural centers of the Anasazi at Chaco Canyon, Mesa Verde, and Kayenta became more sharply distinguished at this time. In these favored spots people gathered in the largest numbers, and each in its own way brought the centuries of growth that were Anasazi to its brightest expression.

The earliest florescence of Anasazi into the full bloom of Classic Pueblo came in a small, narrow valley known as Chaco Canyon. Through countless millennia the Chaco River had shaped and flattened an area eight miles long and little more than a mile wide between the abrupt sandstone cliffs. Here the Anasazi began building great cities as early as A.D. 950; before they were finished, twelve major pueblos and over four hundred small clutches of houses would cover the river valley and adjacent mesa tops. By 1100 most of the buildings had reached their maximum size, and the tiny valley and nearby mesas were supporting a population of about 7,000 people.

At a time when other Anasazi were groping through Developmental Pueblo, the Chacoans were building the largest pueblos the plateau would ever see. The size of the structures bespeaks a high level of social organization, as does the fact that so many people could live compatibly in such close proximity. They must have been farmers and hunters of an extraordinary efficiency to produce enough to feed such a large population, and yet, even under the duress of such a fundamental obligation, the Chacoans found time to raise the creation of pottery and jewelry to new pinnacles of artistry and skill.

In the heart of Chaco Canyon, on the north side of the river and spreading out from the sandstone cliffs, is the sprawling walled city of Pueblo Bonito, the largest community in the canyon and the Southwest. Pueblo Bonito, which means "Beautiful Village," covered more than three acres of ground and rose to a height of four and five stories in places. There were more than eight hundred rooms within the walls, and at the peak of its glory probably a thousand people called Pueblo Bonito home. The sheer size of the building and the magnitude of the construction the Chacoans undertook are difficult to grasp, although it might help to know that Bonito was the largest "apartment house" in the world until 1882, when a bigger one was built in New York City. Although extraordinary in its size, Pueblo Bonito was typical of Chaco pueblos in most features of construction and design.

On the basis of tree-ring dates taken from timbers at Bonito, it is apparent that construction began about A.D. 920, more than a full century before Anasazi to the north and west began making pretensions to this kind of grandeur. More striking than the early date, perhaps, is the fact that Pueblo Bonito was planned from the beginning, and for 150 years, succeeding generations built to fit the conception of the original designers.

Bonito was laid out in a looping horseshoe shape around a central plaza, the rows of rooms rising one story with each succeeding row toward the rear, giving the impression of a carefully terraced amphitheater. Across the front, enclosing the plaza, a row of single-story rooms tied the ends of the horseshoe together. For a people with a keen sense of community it was the ideal building, because the plaza and the rooftops of the entire village—the twin centers of activity—were visible from any point in the pueblo.

Down in the plaza and in the first tier of rooms were the kivas. In addition to the standard clan kivas, which were rarely larger than twenty-five feet in diameter, there were two much larger great kivas, located in the plaza.

Built along the style of the clan kivas but ranging in diameter from forty to sixty feet, these were probably used in ceremonies that demanded the presence of the entire community, or perhaps men from all the surrounding pueblos. Although Bonito's kivas were built above the ground, the subterranean effect was maintained by constructing rooms all around the kiva and filling in any empty spaces with earth. Access still had to be gained from above.

In Pueblo Bonito, as in the rest of Chaco Canyon and the surrounding territory that fell under Chacoan influence, the stone walls were erected by a method that resulted in probably the most beautiful facades in the Southwest. The massive walls were of a three-ply construction: an inner and an outer facing veneer of carefully laid sandstone, with an interior of loose stone rubble and adobe. The veneers were made of flat slices of stone, often smaller than the builder's hand, and laid to a meticulously tight fit. Larger stone blocks were built in courses into the face, often forming linear patterns that added texture and interest to the surface. After all of this careful and attractive masonry was completed, it was covered with a smoothly plastered layer of *caliche* mud.

Heavy beams set into the walls supported floors above ground level, and roofs were fashioned after Anasazi tradition—beams laid across with poles, then brush, followed by a layer of clay or dirt. The beams came from the stands of ponderosa pine that once were scattered over the canyon and mesas—trees long since gone, the victims of relentless harvesting by the Indians for timber and fuel, prevented from regrowth by a subsequent climate change in the region.

Fires were seldom built inside the rooms, as cooking was a task generally reserved for the rooftops and plazas, but doors, windows, and hatchways in the roofs provided the necessary ventilation when a few coals were needed to keep off the chill. The interior rooms with no direct access to outside ventilation were usually used for storage. Late in Pueblo Bonito's life most of the doors and windows opening on the outside wall were sealed up with stone, as was the entrance gate, hinting at some threat from human enemies. Entrance was thereafter gained by ladder, which could be withdrawn in the face of hostile attackers.

For all their careful planning, the builders of Pueblo Bonito made one curious error. Behind one section of the high back wall a tremendous freestanding pillar of standstone was precariously balanced, and the Chacoans recognized its potential for havoc because they periodically replaced the rock and stone that annual rains eroded away from its base. For added security, *pahos*, or prayer sticks, were also thrust under the rock, presumably to provide a theological buttressing for their secular stonework. The effort was successful, for the "Threatening Rock," as early archaeologists called it, did not fall until 1941—after responsibility for the village had long since passed from the hands of the Anasazi to the United States government. When the pillar fell, the worst fears of the Chacoans were realized; it took out a hundred feet of wall and buried thirty rooms.

Another puzzling aspect of Pueblo Bonito is the dearth of burials; archaeologists have found only enough burial sites to account for about 5 percent of the population. There is probably nothing sinister in the fact, but since the Anasazi did not cremate their dead and often buried the dead in trash mounds and other places where the digging was easy, it is unusual that more have not been found. Graves that have been uncovered have yielded large quantities of fine pottery, jewelry, and tools, indicating a sincere respect for the dead person and a concern for the quality of his afterlife.

Pottery in Chaco Canyon followed the traditional Anasazi pattern of black-on-white, with bright white slips and black designs laid on in mineral paints. The decorations were predominantly irregular geometric patterns

Quite different from traditional Anasazi pottery, these bird effigies show the marked influence of Hohokam and Mexican traditions in the Tonto area where they were found.

with bold outlining and fine-lined cross-hatching. Corrugated culinary ware was the rule, and vessels were the usual shapes, although some jugs took human and animal forms.

As jewelers, the Chacoans outshone all their neighbors. From olivella shell and stone they fashioned bead necklaces and pendants of birds and animals. With turquoise, they made mosaics of inlaid bits and strung necklaces using thousands of carefully crafted beads. The delicacy of the work would be difficult to match even with modern steel tools, yet the Chacoans accomplished it with rough-finished stone implements.

The most outstanding characteristic of the Chacoans, though, must have been their skill at intercity diplomacy. With so many people squeezed into such a small area, rivalries surely developed. Even with the primitive irrigation that was practiced—the control of run-off water from melting snows and summer rains—the valley and nearby mesas would have had a difficult time producing enough food for seven thousand people, and somebody must necessarily have had the best land. Since the people at Chaco Canyon were constantly communicating through an elaborate network of roads and trails, and since there is no evidence to indicate intercity warfare, they must have evolved a peaceful system for adjudicating disputes—unless the notion of fighting simply never entered their heads.

The Anasazi of the Mesa Verde, high on the tableland northeast of the Four Corners, tasted the triumph of Classic Pueblo much later than their precocious brethren from Chaco Canyon. In a more typical expression of the pace of events, the Mesa Verde Anasazi began to show signs of the transition about A.D. 1100. The first manifestation of change was the herding instinct of the people, as they abandoned the hundreds of tiny settlements that were sprinkled over the Mesa and began congregating in fewer—and consequently larger—pueblos. These communities, typified by sites like Farview, grew out and up, sometimes as high as four stories. Unlike Pueblo Bonito, most were not planned but grew by accretion, gathering rooms and size at random as the population increased.

The large pueblos tended to rise up in the central zone of the mesa, while villages to the south were abandoned. This trend was apparently the result of a drought which settled on the land between A.D. 1090 and 1101. Rainfall is heavier toward the northern part of the mesa, but on the northernmost reaches the soil thins out and becomes poor; the Anasazi did the sensible thing and resettled where they could get a little of both moisture and fertility.

Initially, the great pueblos were built along traditional Mesa Verde lines, with the kivas out in front of the main dwellings. Very early on, however, the Anasazi began enclosing the kivas within the circle of houses and walls. As the residents of Pueblo Bonito had done, they stopped building doors and windows into the outside ground-floor walls and sealed up those that already existed. The implication is clear: they were providing a first line of defense against attack by outsiders.

The kivas had to be moved inside because of their particular vulnerability. The men of the village under sudden assault could emerge only one at a time, head first and blinking in the bright sunlight, to be finished off individually by one well-positioned attacker with a club. Stone towers several stories high began to appear early in the period, often linked by a tunnel with more exposed kivas, and it has been theorized that these were watchtowers and citadels. Such may have been the case, although these structures might just as easily have fulfilled a ceremonial function; some were located ideally for lookouts, while others were not. Perhaps they served a dual function, or different towers existed for separate and distinct purposes. For the present they remain as just another piece of the puzzle that does not fit neatly anywhere.

Whether building house, kiva, or tower, the Mesa Verde Anasazi brought a new level of achievement to their stone masonry. Walls were often fashioned of a single thickness of rock, the large, rectangular sandstone blocks carefully chipped into symmetry with stone tools. Using an absolute minimum of adobe mortar, these skilled masons stacked the blocks in evenly balanced layers. Even the exposed face was chipped down to give a rustic regularity to the surface—a curious attention to detail, given that a layer of mud plaster covered all of the stonework inside and out. As in their pottery, the Anasazi had transcended mere utility; now not only did something have to work well, it also had to look good in the process.

After only a scant hundred years on the mesa top, the Anasazi of the Mesa Verde began another move, this one even more abrupt than the last. About A.D. 1200 they began moving down over the rimrock and back into the caves—back to what may have been the ancestral Basket Maker home. The relocation must have been made for reasons of defense, because even without considering the work involved in building anew, the caves were clearly inferior places to live: they were difficult to get to; they limited the size and plan of a village; they were shielded from the sun for a good part of the day, making them colder and damper; and they were a poor place to raise rambunctious children and turkeys.

Despite the fact that the Anasazi were in retreat when the cliff dwellings were built, these structures at Mesa Verde are probably the best known of Anasazi ruins. This is in large measure the result of the overhang of the caves, which protected the buildings from natural attrition by rain and snow, which reduced the mesa-top buildings to mounds of random rock. In all other respects the dwellings were unexceptional, merely villages forced to face one direction and shaped in their growth by the cave's existing contours.

The cliff dwellings generally showed little sign of the planning and symmetry that characterized the mesa-top villages, an almost impossible task in light of the limitations imposed by the irregular shape of the cave walls and floor. Some of the masonry was decidedly inferior to earlier work on the mesa top, but this was a natural result when workmen built under the pressure of necessity. When a man needed a place right now to hide his family from marauders, graceful craftsmanship had to be abandoned. This cruder masonry was not readily apparent, however, for the smooth patina of adobe plaster that covered the walls also covered the signs of haste and sacrificed craftsmanship.

Some of the cliff dwellings reached impressive sizes—such as Cliff Palace, with its 200 rooms and 23 kivas—but the rooms were generally smaller than those of the freestanding pueblos. The dark, irregularly shaped rooms at the rear usually served for storage of surplus corn, while the square cubicles facing to the front were family living quarters. The towers, both square and round, persisted in the caves, and the kivas that ranged across the front of the cave exhibited a formalized and rigid similarity. T-shaped doors were built, apparently because their narrow-bottom, wide-top configuration not only reduced the draft in the room but also provided easier defense against intruders.

The decline in craftsmanship necessitated by haste did not extend to ceramics; in fact, Mesa Verde pottery probably became more beautiful after the move to the cliffs. The classic black-on-white persisted, but the techniques of slipping and polishing were refined until the white background often took on a pearlescent quality. The black designs, now rendered totally in vegetable paints, were intricate, repeating geometric patterns, laced with banding and large areas of solid color. It was distinctive and probably the finest expression in black-on-white ever achieved. The high achievement in decorative skills was not completely reflected in vessel manufacture though; there seems to have been a modest decline at this time in the shaping and smoothing of the clay itself.

Even after the move to the cliffs, the Mesa Verde Anasazi continued to farm the mesa tops, but irrigation projects, begun in late Developmental Pueblo times and maintained through the earlier phase of Classic Pueblo, were generally abandoned. These projects ranged from simple check dams on the ravines to reservoirs at Mummy Lake and Morfield. The Mummy Lake system consisted of check dams and collecting ditches to fill the reservoir, and three and a half miles of ditch to transport the water down Chapin Mesa when it was needed. After the move to the cliffs, irrigation efforts deteriorated, and the Anasazi returned to relying solely on their influence with the Almighty.

The third great cultural center of the San Juan drainage system was Kayenta, with its focal point in Tsegi Canyon, where Keet Seel and Betatakin are found. These sites had the distinction of being the last large pueblos in the San Juan to be abandoned. The Anasazi of Kayenta farmed the bottomlands of Tsegi Canyon, but the earth apparently did not produce with the abundance of Chaco or Mesa Verde, for the population remained low, and craftsmanship did not exhibit the attention to detail that leisure time imparts.

Building occurred in both open sites and cliffs, and masonry was decidedly inferior to Chaco and Mesa Verde. Irregularly shaped stones placed at random and packed with great quantities of adobe were typical of the state of the art. Walls made of wattle-and-daub often existed side-by-side with stonework, and pithouses typical of Modified Basket Maker times were occasionally built contemporaneously with, and adjacent to, masonry pueblos.

Kivas represent another departure from the San Juan tradition, for though examples in most open sites and in some caves were circular, they lacked the pilaster roof supports. Some circular kivas were built at Keet Seel, but there were also square, aboveground cere-monial structures, with the traditional kiva floor plan but entered by a door rather than an air shaft; these were called *kihus*. At the cliff dwelling of Betatakin, the kiva was dispensed with and only kihus were built.

The pottery of Kayenta was distinctive, and although corrugated ware was often crude, the decorated pots were well executed. The traditional Anasazi black-on-white was well slipped, and the black designs generally laid on in such a bold and profuse fashion that it often appeared to be white-on-black.

The people of Kayenta also introduced a new wrinkle to San Juan pottery with polychrome designs. Using techniques vaguely reminiscent of the Hohokam, the Kayentans laid down a basic slip of yellow or orange and added the design in white, red, and black. With this strikingly beautiful innovation, the people of Kayenta more than made amends for their shortcomings in architecture.

The influence of the Anasazi cultural centers not only reached out around themselves, but also stretched far away to the south. Encountering established cultures like the Hohokam and Mogollon, the influences mixed to create yet other cultures. Such an encounter explains the origins of the Salado, who moved in among the Hohokam on the Middle Gila, bringing the gospel of surface pueblos. The result was great adobe structures in the desert, such as Casa Grande.

Probably the most striking example of this cultural amalgam was the Sinagua in the area of Flagstaff. Before A.D. 1000 the Sinagua (meaning "without water") were showing signs in their pithouses, pottery, metates, and trinkets of the influences of Hohokam, Mogollon, and Anasazi. But the pattern was intensified by the caprice of Mother Nature when she blew the top off Sunset Crater and showered the surrounding area with volcanic ash. The ash provided an excellent moisture-holding mulch, which tremendously increased the fertility of the soil, and when the word spread, the Southwest's first land rush was on.

Indians pouring in from every direction brought their cultural baggage, and Sinagua blossomed as a fetching, if slightly confused hybrid. At sites like Wupatki, multistoried stone pueblos of Anasazi extraction were built, with walls repeating the three-ply construction of Chaco Canyon. Stone-lined pithouses were built in some locations, and kivas were interpreted in a variety of ways, from circular surface structures to subterranean rectangles, and everything in between. Alongside Wupatki a Hohokam ball court was built, certainly for sport and possibly for ceremonial purposes.

Pottery, the achaeologist's best aid in tracing cultural migration, became very mixed. At Wupatki the most common method for shaping clay was the Hohokam paddle-and-anvil technique, but for decoration the Sinagua seemed to favor the Anasazi black-on-white. This did not preclude them, however, from indulging in a little Mogollon red-on-buff, Hohokam red, or Gila polychrome.

A drought forced the Sinagua out of Wupatki and the surrounding villages in 1225, but they carried their new culture with them into the Tonto Basin, the Verde Valley, and other regions of more reliable water. Thus, some elements of Anasazi culture had begun to spread to the rest of the Southwest even before the Anasazi abandoned their homes and took up the task firsthand.

Even with all the ruins that mark their presence, the pottery that traced their migrations and influences, and the tools that tell of developing civilizations, what we know of the Anasazi is severely limited. From burial remains it is known that they were a short people who deformed their heads, that the women cut their hair short, and that they suffered from arthritis and related bone diseases. Dental problems plagued them constantly, partly the result of the *mano* and *metate* corn grinders that left grit in the meal, which quickly wore down the enamel and opened the teeth to decay. Children probably held a special place in society, for if they died young, they were often buried in a corner of the house, close by the living mother. Burials also reveal that the aged and crippled members of the community were provided for long after they ceased to be productive contributors to society.

They were religious people, and judging from the inflexible design standards of the kiva, in some areas religion was very formalized and codified. Because they were farmers, religion was probably designed to elicit divine intervention in bringing rain and forestalling crop failures. They were not entirely pragmatic, as aesthetic expression in building and pottery came more into evidence as time and agriculture permitted.

They were a peaceful people, who treated amiably with members of their community, close neighbors, and distant groups with whom they carried on sustained trade relations. The communities showed a high level of organization and cooperation in construction of the huge pueblos, the amicable distribution of farm lands, and the existence of the great kivas. This organization probably came at some expense to individual freedom, but since there were no singularly fine and exclusive living quarters to betoken a ruling class, community decisions were probably made in a democratic fashion.

The rapid advance of the Anasazi indicates that they were inventive and adaptable, although not so inventive that they discovered the arch or cantilever construction, and not adaptable enough to prevent their ultimate acquiescence to sustained drought or periodic marauders, or both. Nonetheless, the cultural climb of the Anasazi was an exemplary accomplishment, laced with vigor and spiced with a probing curiosity for the future.

The Dark Wind

The quality of Anasazi life in late Classic Pueblo times was high, compared to the Southwest in general and to earlier stages of development. The Anasazi had acquired all of the necessities of life and even some luxuries: adequate shelter from the elements was available; a regular diet was assured, and food was often plentiful; all the tools of efficient homemaking and hunting were at hand; there was enough leisure time to develop the arts that gave expression to the aesthetic side of their nature; and society was orderly, even to the point of regimentation. All this, and more, contributed to the making of a good and full life, but it did not come cheaply. The lifeway that was Anasazi was bought at the expense of long hours of hard work, and it was not without its discomforts. Although the Anasazi accepted the necessary sacrifices, hard work was not enough to preserve the world their ancestors had worked so long to establish.

Late in the thirteenth century a dark wind of mysterious origins swept across the San Juan, driving the Anasazi from their ancestral homeland. By 1300 most of the cities and villages of the northern plateau were abandoned, for reasons that are not quite clear. Perhaps the scourge upon the land was a long, sustained drought which withered the crops and left the Anasazi starving. Possibly it was the pressure of marauding, warlike Shoshonean raiders, taking advantage of the Anasazi tradition of peace. Whatever the source, it was a compelling force that sent the ancient builders of the San Juan forever from their homes.

The life of a farmer, working the stingy soils of the semiarid Southwest with stone tools, was not easy. The season was long, often running from late March through the end of October, and for part of the season it was a twenty-four-hour-a-day job. It demanded total commitment, for any malingering could mean partial or complete failure of the crop—which, in turn, threatened the lives of all those in the community.

Taking the example of Mesa Verde, a farmer's year normally began in late March, after the winter snows had melted off the mesa top. The first job was clearing new land and breaking up the soil of established fields. While the ground was still damp and fires were easy to control, the farmers began burning off the large trees in virgin soil and chopping out the brush with stone axes. With the land clear they set about breaking up the compacted earth with stone-tipped digging sticks, loosening the soil down as much as a foot, not only to allow planting but also to permit the soil to soak up as much water as possible.

Planting began in early May, after the last frost (it was hoped) and before the first warm rains of late spring. If planted too early, the budding shoots would be killed by the cold, and if planted after the rain, the crop would lose the advantage of heavy moisture during sprouting. Corn was planted in bunches on little hillocks, often as many as a dozen grains buried a foot deep to take the greatest advantage of available moisture. Once the seed was in the ground, the farmer wrung his hands waiting for the first—and usually last—heavy rain before a long, dry summer.

After the rain the farmers settled down to a summer of daily weeding and constant vigilance. Most of the creatures that walked, crawled, or flew on the Mesa Verde found growing corn, beans, and squash an irresistible temptation. All day the men picked off bugs, chased birds, and matched wits with squirrels and rabbits and deer. At night the young men and boys of the village took over the job, battling not only the animals but their own fear as well.

For the women the spring and summer were an equally busy time. Barred by the cold from making pots during the winter, this was the time to replace all of the broken pieces. It was a time-consuming task, but jugs and pots were essential for storing food through the winter and often water through the summer. Each spring the women laid in a supply of water, to be stored in the dark recesses of the caves for use during a dry summer. If the summer proved too long and dry, they began making daily treks to distant springs, carrying heavy loads of water up the steep cliffs. In addition, there were winter clothes to be made and mended, often houses to be replastered, and the constant obligation to set at least two square meals a day before the family.

The farmers continued to worry their way through the summer until late July, when the light rains began again—provided their ceremonial toils in the kivas had been successful. The weeding and animated scarecrowing continued until late August, when the harvest began. Every day through the end of October, the men harvested the mature corn and the women worked at drying and storing it for the coming winter. Fall was also the time to gather wild nuts and berries, which likewise had to be prepared for storage.

After the harvest, with the coming of colder weather, the game began moving back down from the high country. The men immediately began to spend their days stalking the deer and mountain sheep of the mesa, while the women turned to the task of cleaning and butchering the take, and following that, drying the meat and dressing the skins for use as garments.

The arrival of winter with the December snows spelled the end of days filled with long hours of work, but it was not a time anticipated with any glee. The cliff dwellings were cold and dank during the winter, usually warmed for only a few hours every day by the sun, and colds and arthritic pain were constant companions of many in the village. The cold struck hardest at the women and children, because they spent their nights huddled in rooms without fires and their days crouched around fires on the rooftops. In the tiny, poorly ventilated rooms, fires were out of the question for all but the most desperate, and they paid for the warmth by choking on the smoke. The men, on the other hand, spent most of their time in the kivas, even sleeping there. Because of the ventilator system, fires could be kept burning in the snug subterranean nests, so the men spent most of the winter out of the cold wind and close by a warming fire.

It was not an easy life, except possibly for the men during the winter, and even they suffered the dull, bland diet that dried foods dictated—and it could get even harder if the rains failed to come and there was no harvest or small game. But the Anasazi managed to cope with it, even to thrive on it, because it was the best they had, and it was their own. Even so, time was running out for the people of the Mesa Verde, and for all the Anasazi of the San Juan.

Toward the end of the thirteenth century, the Anasazi began to leave their homes in the San Juan region of the plateau. There was no mass exodus, but one by one the cities and villages were abandoned until by 1300 there was no one left. No clear-cut explanation for the departure is apparent, but it must have been a compelling reason to force these settled and established town builders from the only land they knew.

It is obvious that the Anasazi had been increasingly threatened over the last several hundred years by some force of hostile outsiders. The threat can be seen in the growing defensive nature of the pueblos: walls became more massive and were extended to provide a solid barrier to the outside; the vulnerable kivas were brought inside the compound, and often linked to highly defensible towers; and the doors and windows on the outside walls at ground level were filled in solidly with stone and mortar. This defensive posture culminated in the move to the cliff dwellings, as at Mesa Verde, or the erection of stone towers to guard all vulnerable approaches to the village, as at Hovenweep.

The threat probably came from nomadic Shoshoneans, the hunting and gathering tribes of the Great Basin who were roving into the plateau country about this time. For protection of life and limb the defenses of the villages were probably adequate against these fierce raiders, as the nomads had neither the tools nor the temperament to breech defended walls or sustain a lengthy siege. Also, there is little sign of pitched battles or massacres.

The raiders naturally suffered other disadvantages as well. They would be attacking cities of large population, whose residents were not only physically fit from hard labor in the fields but were probably better fed, and therefore stronger, than the attackers. Raiding parties large enough to outnumber the villagers would be easily detected, and the attackers would lose the essential element of surprise. The villagers also enjoyed the advantage of superior organization and discipline, a factor probably more important than any other in warfare.

While there is little likelihood that nomadic raiders could successfully attack a prepared village, they could play hob with the precious crops in the field. At the first sign of attack, the traditionally peaceful Anasazi farmers would flee their fields for the safety of the pueblo-cum-fortress. A few men might be lost in a surprise assault, but the greatest tragedy would come in the fields. The raiders could plunder a ripened crop at will, stealing all the food they could carry and, if they had a particularly mean streak, burning the rest. The effect of such a raid on a village's morale would be devastating, for to sit helplessly by while a whole year's work disappeared in a single stroke could help no farmer's pride or enthusiasm for the job. If the raids continued year after year, the effect on the village's food reserves would be catastrophic. In short, while the raiders could not push the villagers out by force of arms, they could, by whittling at the food supply with quick, predatory raids, make the Ancient Ones want to leave.

Another factor which may have caused the departure—the one archaeologists generally like to cite as the root cause—is the severe drought that befell the entire plateau late in the thirteenth century. Close study of tree-ring data used in dating the ruins reveals abnormally narrow growth rings between the years 1276 and 1299, indicating that an unrelieved drought spanned those years. (Although there probably was a drought, it should be pointed out that tree-ring analysis is not infallible. Narrow growth rings can also be caused when an adequate amount of moisture exists but excessively low temperatures prevail. Additionally, it should be remembered that tree growth is largely determined by the amount of winter precipitation, as moisture from the snowfall seeps down and is stored deep near the root system, while crop growth is more a function of summer rainfall.)

If the drought was as severe and unrelenting as the tree rings seem to indicate, the effect on the Anasazi was predictable. Normally they could store a reserve of corn to last two or three years, before they had eaten their way down to the precious seed corn. If they were forced to eat that, they were finished as farmers unless more corn for planting could be borrowed, bought, or stolen from someone else. A drought would also diminish the other sources of food that normally supplemented the crops from their fields. Wild berries and piñon nuts would shrivel or fail to mature in the driving heat, and as the natural foliage and grasses disappeared from lack of moisture, large and small game would move out of the region in search of graze.

In areas where the Anasazi farmed the flat river valleys along perpetually live streams, under conditions like those at Chaco Canyon, a severe drought was not necessary to cause difficulties. In these areas the farmers relied on irrigation to water their fields, diverting flood water flow onto the crops. But during periods of even moderately reduced rainfall the rivers began cutting deep arroyos, eating away at the streambed, and gradually lowering their own level. The water level soon dropped below the level of the fields, so it could no longer be diverted by gravity for irrigation. Not only was water lost to the farmers, but the arroyo-cutting often carved huge gashes through their fields on the fertile bottomlands.

While the drought theory is logical and has the authority of general acceptance, there are certain inconsistencies that blemish its credibility. Probably most important is the fact that if the tree-ring analysis is accepted, the Anasazi survived earlier droughts of similar intensity and duration. In some cases the Anasazi who abandoned their San Juan homes moved to areas that modern analysis has shown to have even less rainfall than the region departed, an example being Antelope Mesa. If they were escaping only a drought, it would seem logical to move to the area of greatest rainfall, which is along the eastern end of the Mogollon Rim. Unfortunately, none of the Anasazi ever settled there.

In all probability the Anasazi were the victims of an unusual combination of circumstances, which taken in concert were too much for them to endure. A long, hard drought they could deal with, as they had in the past, and although times might be lean, they could survive. Similarly, raiders might be dangerous if they caught a man in his fields, or frustrating if they destroyed the crops and reduced the village to short rations, but there was no way they could kill a fortified civilization by assaulting the villages. Either of these problems, capable of solution by the Anasazi, was not enough to drive them out of their home; but together, each chipping away at confidence and resolve, they may have proved more than the Anasazi could cope with.

It has been suggested that the arrival of hard times and competition for the diminished resources bred quarreling and strife among the Anasazi, adding further to the disintegration of the ancestral communities or even inciting inter-Pueblo warfare. While this is possible, there is no real evidence of internecine warfare, and it is a condition that contradicts many centuries of growing community life and cooperation.

Flute player and shield, Galisteo Basin, New Mexico.

RIO GRANDE ANCIENTS

The humpbacked flute player is a deity rooted deep in Anasazi traditions and is still rampant in the pantheons of many pueblo peoples. To the Hopi he is Kokopelli, influential in fertility and abundance, whether it be in the hunt, the fields, or human reproduction. Thus his presence in the Galisteo Basin of the Rio Grande country is natural, for the region was a place of rebirth for the Anasazi and other Southwest peoples. Along the drainage of the Rio Grande and over the Sangre de Cristo divide in the Pecos valleys, the wandering Anasazi who were pried loose from their ancestral homes found fertile soil for the old ways and settled in to try again.

The restless migrations that characterized the pueblo peoples after A.D. 1300 spawned many of the Rio Grande pueblos that survive today, and reinforced the populations of those already existing. From north, south, and west they brought the rudiments and regional refinements of their lifeways, blending them peacefully in a common urge to re-create life as they had known it. Thus it was that the pueblo of Pecos arose, which survived into the first half of the nineteenth century and which provided the inspiration for pioneer archaeologist Adolf Bandelier's probing humanistic novel of ancient pueblo life, *The Delight Makers.* In the mountain country surrounding the Rito de los Frijoles now known as Bandelier National Monument, also within the Rio Grande region, Anasazi efforts at reconstructing their lives were less permanent.

The Rio Grande remains today a living center for the remnants of the ancient ways, from Taos Pueblo in the north to Isleta Pueblo south of Albuquerque. And further south still rise the ruins of Gran Quivira and Gila—Mogollon peoples grown into Anasazi, who played out their string in their homeland as heirs to the Ancient Ones before moving to join the surviving groups who had settled along the Rio Grande.

Overleaf: Abandoned mission church and kiva stand in lonely counterpoint in Pecos National Monument.

The adobe ruin of the mission church preaches the lesson that it is indeed the earth that abides. The conflict of world views, triggered by missionary zeal, resulted in success for neither Spaniard nor Indian, and left a measure of failure for both.

The deteriorating walls of Pueblo de las Humanas were once a center of population and power, but they never sheltered the jewels and gold that lured Coronado here to Gran Quivira.

154

A kiva on the cliffs above the Rito de los Frijoles in Bandelier National Monument marks an attempt by the gypsy bands of Anasazi to restore the world they were forced to leave. In this region diverse peoples of the stone village tradition met to mix their heritages in the emerging pan-pueblo amalgam.

Tyuonyi ruin on the floor of Canyon Rito de los Frijoles was a closed bastion with labyrinthine entries and a dearth of kivas, hinting that perhaps physical fear overrode spiritual tradition.

Far to the south, close to the strong influences out of Mexico, the Mimbres people developed skills in animistic representation that were not to be surpassed.

Effigy of mother and child, from the pueblo ruin of Casas Grandes in northern Sonora, Mexico. The artistic techniques and skill that made their way north were repaid by building ideas of Anasazi origin that filtered down to the south.

With rooms crouched low in the bosom of the rock, the style and essence
of pueblo cliff dwelling were quickly adopted by the desert people of
the upper Gila when touched by the spreading Anasazi influence.

A Mimbres bowl design in black-on-white. Although in many respects the technological heirs of the Anasazi, the Mimbres transcended in artistry all preceding potters.

Right: The metamorphosis of spring adorns the narrow-leaf yucca with delicate wands. Below: Gila Cliff Dwellings, where the Anasazi lifeway met the challenge of the desert.

Into the Memory

The Anasazi, who gradually abandoned the scattered villages and great cultural centers on the northern plateau, did not simply walk out into the sands of the southern desert and disappear, vaporizing like the morning dew. They were a people escaping—from precisely what we cannot be sure—and they fanned out across the land like so many gypsies, carrying a few possessions on their backs and the cultural heritage of a thousand years in their heads. They went in search of new homes, scattering in groups large and small, usually heading east, south, and west toward the familiar trading territory of their halcyon days. Some of them built new villages in likely-looking spots; others made their way to communities pioneered along the Rio Grande by fiddle-footed Anasazi hundreds of years earlier; and still others found their way among other Southwest cultures, such as the Salado, Sinagua, and shades in between, who had already felt the influence of Anasazi and lived a life that was recognizable, though different in many details, to the migrants.

It was a time of great unrest in much of the Southwest, not just for the Anasazi, but for the Sinagua, Salado, Hohokam, and the tattered remnants of Mogollon. Most of the once stable, sedentary farmers and town builders were on the move, pushed by fear, drought, curiosity, or a need for more room. They met, mixed, and moved on, sampling the cultures of others, learning new skills, adopting new traits, and leaving some of their own behind. In time the once distinct cultures would become mixed in a confusing amalgam of styles, traits, and traditions, but out of it would emerge a pan-cultural whole, a lifeway that, though different in detail from area to area, we know as Pueblo.

The Anasazi swept into this cultural maelstrom, contributing to it in no small part themselves, and began to lose the distinct identity that had developed on the plateau as Anasazi. The purity of the culture gradually eroded, but they poured their building skills, their religion, and their crafts in among the rest to influence the pan-Pueblo lifeway that

Identities emblazoned on their shields, these figures commemorate an ancient battle on the weathered stone of the Galisteo Basin, New Mexico.

survives to today. The Anasazi would never really vanish because they are a part of the genetic and mythic memory of men yet building pueblos of stone and adobe, women still shaping their pottery, and young boys learning their way into manhood in the kivas.

The road was not an easy one, for even as the Anasazi were finding new homes and losing themselves in the changing spectrum of Southwest cultures, a new disruptive force, more terrible in the long run than nomadic raiders or drought, entered their lives. The Spanish appeared, first in 1539, and thereafter in greater numbers, carving an empire and attempting to make facsimile Spaniards of the ancient peoples. It was a time of trial for all the Pueblos, testing the strength and durability of their traditional lifeway against the European institutions that sought to crush and displace it. On the heels of the Spaniards came the Americans, with a similar resolve, and it is a testament to roots sunk deep in two thousand years of Anasazi, Mogollon, and Hohokam tradition that the Pueblo Indians survived at all.

The Anasazi, who departed their plateau homeland to mix and blend among themselves and other cultures, began to settle in three major areas: along the northern reaches of the Rio Grande and at two major centers in the drainage of the Little Colorado River, one at Zuñi and the other at the foot of Black Mesa among the Hopi towns. In each of the areas they were not so much witnesses to the demise of their old culture, as midwives at the birth of new ones. The cultures that evolved in Rio Grande, Zuñi, and Hopi during the fourteenth and fifteenth centuries are ancestral to the Pueblo cultures that survive in these same areas today.

The Anasazi had laid the groundwork for their migration to the Rio Grande fully three hundred years before the final departure from the San Juan region. By A.D. 1000 a recognizable, if retarded, Basket Maker Anasazi culture had begun to emerge near the Rio Grande. Although it never reached the development seen at Chaco Canyon or Mesa Verde, this Anasazi satellite fashioned the traditional black-on-white pottery and learned to build with adobe and stone. As it matured, other influences began to appear out of the west and south, and under the stimulus of the migrations in the late thirteenth century, a major cultural center began to emerge.

About 1300 the population of the Rio Grande valley increased suddenly, a consequence of the movement away from the northern plateau. As a result of this extraordinary growth, the largest pueblos ever built in the region were constructed, some numbering hundreds of rooms. Construction varied with time and place, but the general tendency was toward fewer and larger pueblos—apparently the herd instinct had not been lost. Pueblos followed the traditions developed at Chaco Canyon and on the mesa tops of Mesa Verde, as masses of rooms, often multileveled, were arranged around a central, protected plaza. Masonry was sometimes the medium, especially in the northernmost pueblos, but solid adobe or mixed adobe and stone construction was as often the case south of Santa Fe or Albuquerque. Kivas also reflected the varied influences, as they ranged from chambers above the ground and incorporated into room blocks, to subterranean square and circular rooms located in the plazas. Some had ventilators, deflectors, and firepits, but quite often they lacked the stone pilasters that were an integral part of Anasazi kivas.

Pottery also began to change amid the confluence of cultural traditions. The predominantly black-on-white patterns began to be replaced by red-slipped, oxidized ware, and pots' shapes and decorative designs reflected an almost infinite variety of choices. Hard, shiny glazes, introduced initially in the west, found their way to the Rio Grande and marked the beginning of a degenerative trend in pottery making. As time wore on, the glazes, never used as full slips but only for decoration, became sloppy and haphazard. It was not

162

Historic Zuñi owl figures carry on the long black-on-white tradition.

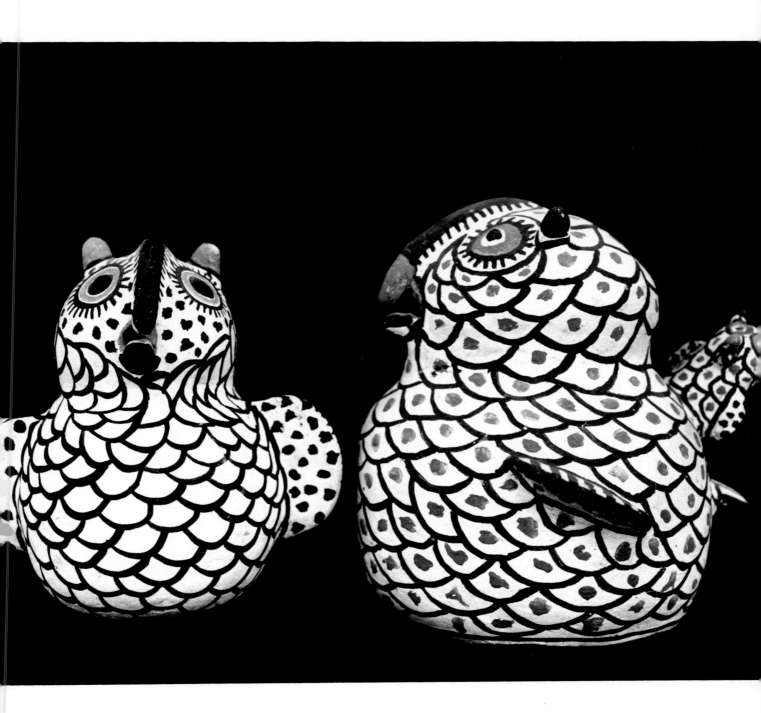

until the seventeenth century that glazing was dropped in favor of a return to dull red slips and black paints. The traditional corrugated culinary ware gave way to plain black pottery, and in the northern Rio Grande there appeared a thick, heavy, often crumbly pottery called biscuit ware, which was predominantly gray with crude black designs.

Some of the Anasazi making the move toward the Rio Grande did not make it in one jump but paused along the way to try their luck with new cities. One such attempt gave rise to Tyuonyi at Rito de los Frijoles, of present-day Bandelier National Monument. A large masonry pueblo, probably several stories high and circular, was built and occupied for about a hundred years after 1420. In the center of the plaza three circular and subterranean clan kivas were built, while outside the walls was situated a great kiva. The cliffs above Tyuonyi were pockmarked with tiny caves, many of them extensively hollowed out for habitation and partially walled across the front opening. Unfortunately, the builders of Tyuonyi and the many other villages in the region did not have the easily shaped sandstone of their old homeland with which to work, and they settled instead for the broken and jagged pieces of lava and tuff (consolidated volcanic ash and cinders) which abound in the area. The resulting masonry is not nearly so pleasing as the much older handiwork of the Anasazi in the San Juan.

The Bandelier region was apparently the meeting ground for a number of cultural strains, all of which failed to take hold with any permanence. As a result, the region abounds in tentative efforts to adapt old techniques to new surroundings, and the results of cultures meeting and mixing. One example of this is the Stone Lions of Cochiti, a hunting shrine on top of a mesa ten miles from Tyuonyi. Two large stone effigies of mountain lions, carved out of solid rock and surrounded by a wall, crouch in mute inscru-

tability. They had no precedent among the Anasazi and were probably the unique fallout of a singular cultural collision.

In the western cultural centers of Hopi and Zuñi, as in the case of the Rio Grande, the migrating Anasazi did not wander into a cultural vacuum. The region had long been under the influence of Kayenta, in addition to feeding on the cultural crumbs of Hohokam and the cultural hybrids, Salado and Sinagua. Here, however, the interweaving of traditions did not have the confusing and often debilitating results that seemed to mark some of the Rio Grande experience.

Among the washes and narrow mesa tops at the southern end of Black Mesa which mark the heart of Hopi land, the level of architecture reached a high order soon after 1300. Fine masonry techniques in large houses, often covering an acre or more, were the rule, and in time the larger pueblos would come to cover ten to twelve acres. The layout of the villages often followed a pattern of long rows of buildings laid side by side, with open plaza areas intervening between each. Kivas showed a marked departure from Anasazi tradition, as they were rectangular, normally measuring about ten by fourteen feet. At one end a short bench spanned a niche recessed three feet into the wall, while the ventilator shaft ran under the floor to open near the center of the room. Set in the floor along each side were loom blocks designed to hold warp threads of cotton cloth, indicating that Hopi men wove more than the ceremonial elements of their religion in the kiva.

The Hopi tradition in ceramics leaned heavily on oxidized pottery, resulting in predominantly yellow and orange motifs. Some black-on-white pots were made, but reducing-atmosphere firing never found the high form of expression it once knew on the plateau. Probably the most delightful product of the developing culture in Hopi was the emergence of a finely crafted polychrome pottery early in the fourteenth century. The style, which consisted of red and black designs on a yellow background, persisted until the seventeenth century and resulted in some of the most appealing pottery ever produced in the Southwest.

To the south and east of the Hopi sphere of influence lay Zuñi, the third of the persistent cultural areas. It was among the Zuñi that the use of glazes began, and although the designs in scrolls, squared scrolls, hachuring, and intricate repeating patterns bound between bold outlines were commendable, the effect was destroyed by the glaze paints. Glazes were hard to control during firing, often running or piling in great globs, spoiling the impact of the colors and design.

Among the Zuñi some of the finest architecture of the period is found. Working in sandstone mortared with adobe, they achieved a result strongly reminiscent of the style developed at Chaco Canyon. Similarly, the kivas at Zuñi show a strong debt to Chaco and Mesa Verde, in some instances repeating the traditional pattern almost exactly. The only distinctions are the ventilator opening near the center of the floor and the absence of the stone pilasters, after the fashion of developments late in Chaco Canyon's history.

The new Pueblo cultures that were developing around the Rio Grande and in Hopi and Zuñi might very well have continued to evolve in their established directions, growing more distinctive and dynamic and perhaps transcending the ancestral days of glory, had it not been for the arrival of the Spanish. Clanking ponderously but inexorably northward on the three-legged juggernaut of Spanish civilization—priests, presidios, and *patronés*—the Europeans constituted a disruptive and very nearly destructive presence.

The story began in 1539, when the Franciscan monk Fray Marcos de Niza launched an expedition to the uncharted lands north of New Spain. He was charged with the task of finding the Seven Cities of Cíbola, the mythic cities of gold whose purported existence had been conjured up in the Spanish imagination sometime in the ninth century. The idea was just ridiculous enough to appeal to the conquistadores, and so at each stage of discovery it was assumed that the Seven Cities lay somewhere over the horizon. Fray Marcos was guided by a black Moor named Esteban, whose credentials included an impressive eight-year stint of wandering lost across Texas and New Mexico with Cabeza de Vaca, during which time he developed a familiarity with the land, an ability to communicate by sign language with the natives, and a flair for showmanship.

Esteban proceeded ahead of the van, delighting in the attention he received and the consternation he caused among the Indians with his tales of the emissary from the Great White God who followed him. Unfortunately for Esteban, the Zuñis were unimpressed and killed him. Fray Marcos received word of the murder and, fearful for his own life, only came close enough to glimpse a distant pueblo. Convinced he had seen one of the Seven Cities —probably because that was what he wanted to see—he scurried back to Mexico City with the good news.

His report immediately set in motion another expedition, this time commanded by Coronado and guided by Fray Marcos. The journey was arduous, and by the time Coronado reached the Zuñi village of Hawikuh, he was more interested in food than gold and fought his way in with dispatch. Even so, the disappointment of finding no golden cities, only adobe villages of simple farmers who did not even know what gold was, pushed Coronado over the brink. He was now convinced, after a fashion peculiar to conquistadores, that the Seven Cities must exist and it only remained to find them. Quite likely the Zuñis, in their haste to be rid of him, encouraged the delusion. Coronado took his column to the cluster of villages at Tiguex on the Rio Grande, where he massacred an entire village after trouble developed. Pecos Pueblo also got its first taste of Spanish civilization before Coronado finally gave up and went home.

After leaving the Pueblo Indians unmolested for almost forty years, Spanish expeditions returned and began building the towns, churches, and forts that meant they had come to stay. There were clashes, but the Pueblos were at a hopeless disadvantage against horsemen armed with steel weapons, and the process of subjugation began. The colonizers, regarding the Indians as a ready pool of labor to be exploited in the interest of civilization, set about requisitioning and enslaving as many as possible. Pueblo corn crops were destroyed to make the Indians dependent on the *patronés,* and communities were broken up to destroy what little organization for resistance the Pueblos possessed. The priests were no better, for it was acknowledged by the church that any means necessary to bring enlightenment to the heathen were justified. To make certain that their pagan souls were saved from eternal damnation, the Pueblos were beaten and hanged, and their kivas destroyed. In addition to all the deliberate abuse, the Spaniards brought with them European diseases for which the Pueblos had no natural immunity, and the results were predictably catastrophic.

In 1642 a small uprising occurred, but it died abruptly from lack of organization. Nonetheless, the wounds suffered by the Pueblos' pride and civilization festered just beneath a quiescent exterior, and in 1680 the anger born of pain and humiliation finally burst forth. Despite the distance between villages, the language barrier, and the Pueblo tradition of tending to one's own affairs, a medicine man of Pueblo San Juan named Popé managed to organize a revolt by all the villages from Taos to the Hopi mesas. The Spaniards learned of the conspiracy, and the revolt had to begin prematurely in some areas; but the surprise and unity achieved by the Indians was sufficient to break the back of Spanish colonization in the Southwest. Ultimately, the Spanish had to abandon their last stronghold at Santa Fe, leaving behind some four hundred dead in the entire region. The Pueblos seemed to take a special glee in evening the score with the priests, and in one short night the church acquired a long list of new martyrs, sent to

their rewards in the most grisly fashion.

The Pueblos enjoyed their success for twelve years, steadfastly holding the Spaniards at bay, but the years were not easy ones. In addition to fending off the tentative countermoves of the Spanish, the Pueblos were harassed by the traditionally predatory Utes, Navajos, and Apaches, now grown more dangerous by the fact that they had become horsemen. Also, a drought arrived to plague the already beleaguered Pueblos.

In 1692 Don Diego de Vargas reconquered them and established Spanish dominion over the Southwest. With little more than some judicious propagandizing, to turn suspicious villages against one another, coupled with threats and a show of force, Vargas brought the rebellious Pueblos back under the mantle of Spanish civilization. Interestingly enough, the Hopis, nominally the most peaceful of the Pueblos, were never reconquered.

This was not the end of resistance, for trouble would flare periodically at individual villages, but the Pueblos could never again muster the organization needed to banish the interlopers and return to their old paths unhindered.

The Pueblos could not fully escape the influence of conquering peoples, whether they were Spanish, Mexican, or American. They have adopted many of the wares and tools of industrial society over the years, learned to farm and work in a commercial world, and paid lip service to religions and governments that mean nothing to them. But more than anything else, they have survived essentially intact in the midst of an alien society seemingly antithetical to their own. They have sustained their pueblos and village life, kept sacred the kivas, and maintained a world view uniquely their own. It is a lifeway of tradition, strengthened by time and pride, harmonious with the earth and elements, its roots sunk deep in the bedrock of the ancient plateau.

Hopi Kachina dolls: The masked gods in effigy.

CONTEMPORARY PUEBLOS

The Pueblo Indians who live today in the Hopi villages at the foot of Black Mesa, at Zuñi, and in the pueblos along the Rio Grande carry the blood of the ancients in their veins and follow lives rich in the spirit of a world view nurtured in over two thousand years of tradition. Theirs is a self-image as old as the rock itself, sustained in the recounting of their creation with the world, buttressed by the assurance of their place and role in the infinite cycle of life. They are the people of this land, born to be a part of it, and drawing strength from the whole they have survived.

Over four hundred years ago they began to face the challenge of interlopers whose roots ran no deeper than a footprint, whose understanding of man's place in the natural world focused only with a perspective from the top, and whose regard for the supernatural fluctuated between fear and hypocrisy. Against the steel and gunpowder onslaught of the Spanish, the Pueblos momentarily buckled, although in time they found the strength to strike back. Even when conquered, the strength of deep roots continued to sustain a passive resistance and obdurant adherence to the ancient and balanced ways.

In time the Spanish were replaced by Americans, energetic and enthusiastic newcomers with a tunnel vision for empire so severe that they failed to notice the Pueblos until the native residents started getting in the way of Progress—whereupon the Indians discovered the American solution for obstacles on the land: exterminate and remove. Failing that, the next step was to make the obstacle invisible by the expediency of assimilation. The Pueblos faced their harshest test during the years when the federal government sought to bring the joys of civilization to the primitives and cancel the white man's debt of guilt for years of brutality and double dealing by making white men of the Indians.

Under the corrosive energy and ingenuity of modern America, the tangible elements of Pueblo tradition have been visibly eroded, but in the subterranean bedrock of spiritual values the way of the ancients continues to survive intact—a legacy of oneness with the world, tempered in the experience of the ages.

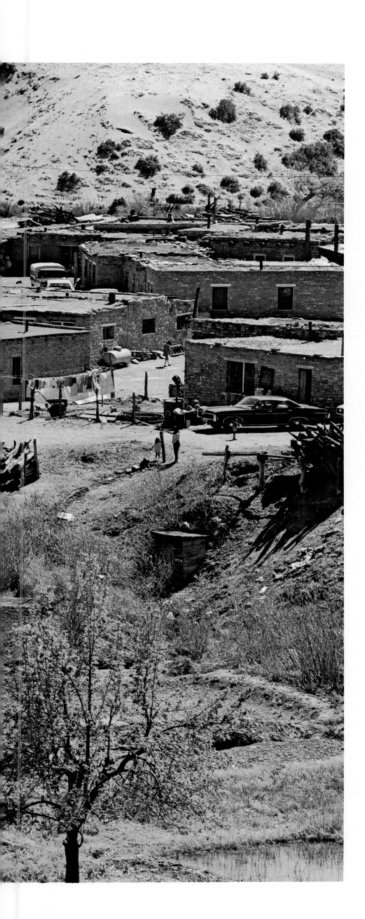

*Left: The Hopi village of Moenkopi. The modern
Pueblo Indian, rooted in the old ways
but resident in a new age, daily faces the
challenge of his identity. Below: The
ancestral staple, grown in the ancient way.*

*Overleaf: North plaza of Taos Pueblo, behind dormant
beehive bread ovens. The same sense of community
and identity with the natural world that once bound
the Anasazi together survives and thrives today.*

Although additional arts have been adopted and perfected, design in pottery remains the foundation of modern Pueblo aesthetic expression, as in this Hopi polychrome.

Winged scroll design in modern Hano polychrome.

The transition to the modern is captured in a Santo Domingo pot crafted after the Spanish conquest.

The pueblo of Ácoma, which reaches
back into prehistory for its origins,
continues life quietly and passively,
preserving the roots and memory of
the ancient ways for those who find
a need.

Ácoma, the Sky City, stands as a living link to the lifeway that was Anasazi.

The Flute Ceremony at the sacred spring below the Mishongnovi mesa (1902).

HISTORIC PHOTOGRAPHS
by Adam Clark Vroman

It might be said that the world of Anasazi disappeared with the people who abandoned the ancestral villages at the end of the thirteenth century, losing their identity and the purity of the lifeway in the cultural amalgam that emerged as Pueblo. But to believe that would be to deny the essential nature of the Anasazi, for they were a dynamic, adaptable people with a strong tradition of growing by sharing with the other cultures of the Southwest. The Anasazi had reached out to teach and to learn all their lives, to such a degree that the pan-Pueblo culture that was born of catastrophe might have arisen naturally from the Anasazi penchant for sharing everyone's cultural advances. In this light the world of the modern Pueblo may be a most accurate reflection of what it meant to be purely Anasazi.

That reflection began to be a subject for photographers toward the end of the nineteenth century, but with few exceptions they missed the essence of the reflection and saw instead only exotic curios, living and breathing museum pieces, or savage and superstitious rituals. One of the few who looked be-

yond the preconceptions of his own society was Adam Clark Vroman, and what he saw was people—truly noble people living in close communion with the natural world, possessed, perhaps, of a clearer understanding of life than he had himself.

There was little in Vroman's background to portend the vision and sensitivity that his work would come to express. He was not a professional photographer, but a highly successful businessman and bookdealer in Pasadena, California, who found himself with the time and money to travel. He went to the Southwest first as a tourist in 1895, taking snapshots like any other visitor. But he was touched by the people whose oneness with the earth and the eternal was singular in an emerging America. Vroman continued his pilgrimages to the Southwest for ten years, ranging the pueblos along the Rio Grande and at Zuñi and Hopi with his large view camera. His written notes about his subjects were sketchy, but he recorded with increasing clarity and sympathy the face, and even part of the soul, of an ancient lifeway.

The celebrated potter Nampeyo firing pottery at Hano (1901).

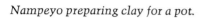
Nampeyo preparing clay for a pot.

Firing pottery at Ácoma (1904).

Hopi woman making plaques at Shungopavi (1901).

Man and woman of Taos (1899).

LEFT: *"Mary" painting pottery at Ácoma (1902).*
BELOW: *A Zuñi man drilling turquoise at Laguna (1904).*

Photographic Notes

Discovering and exploring the Anasazi dwellings of the Southwest has always held a special, magical niche in my mental and photographic wanderings. Whether these ancient peoples realized their architectural creations were capable of such dramatic emotional impact, I don't know. Simple and functional in design, the structures express an almost mystical harmony between man and the land. Each of the photographs in this collection represents visually the fleeting impressions that I was experiencing in the blink of time in which I clicked the shutter. I hope that together they will communicate a poignant awareness of these vanished peoples and their distinctive life-style in the rock.

When beginning my many pilgrimages to canyons and mesas of the Anasazi, I purposely attempted, as best I could, to clear my mind of the usual influences that command creative work today and let my personal response bring a more intense focus on the Anasazi experience. Though I work intuitively, some discipline was needed to meet the challenge of the Anasazi ruins. A photographer always risks the danger of being caught up in the purely pictorial—the spectacular natural forms of the Southwest that hold and surround the ancient dwellings. Since the Anasazi lived a simple everyday life, their structures too presented simple, sweeping forms. Thus it was necessary sometimes to complement those spectacular expanses of sandstone and sky with delicate wall detail or masonry. Wherever possible, photographic techniques were kept simple so as not to impede a straightforward presentation of these ancient structures in the balance and harmony expressed by their builders. In a few instances wide-angle lenses were used, for example, to relate the great kivas in their entirety to show the geometric rhythm of rectangular living quarters and kiva forms in the round. I trust the contemporary reader will accept these few deviations on my part to better achieve a more complete note of expression. Clear focus and a sometimes brooding mood were both important tools to express complex perceptions I felt.

All the photographs were made on Ektachrome daylight film, most of them with a 4x5 Linhof Teknika and a few with a 500 C Hasselblad. Exposures were made from a Weston light meter. Lenses included a 75, 100, 135, 210, 360, and 500mm for the Linhof, a 250 and 500mm for the Hasselblad. Filters, which I use sparingly, were Polarization, 81A, 81B, CC10R, CC10B, CC10G (glass and gelatin), primarily to correct a gap in the relationship between what I feel or perceive and what the film actually sees.

I like to travel light, especially on arduous treks into the wilder places, so carry a limited selection of whatever equipment the situation may call for. However, a tripod was used in all of the work. The more I can forget the intricacies of my equipment, the more I can concentrate on the subject and composition. Ideally the camera becomes an extension of my eye.

—DAVID MUENCH

Photographic Details

PAGES 2–3: Kiva and lower walls of White House ruin, Canyon de Chelly National Monument, Arizona. 75mm Super Angulon.

PAGES 4–5: Storm moods of winter, Farview House, Chapin Mesa, Mesa Verde National Park, Colorado. 100mm Wide-Field Ektar.

PAGES 6–7: Long House ruin interior, Wetherill Mesa, Mesa Verde National Park, Colorado. Ancient fires have sooted this enormous cavity in the sandstone. 135mm Symmar.

PAGE 21: Mesa Verde–type double-handle mug, in collection of Mesa Verde Museum, Mesa Verde National Park, Colorado. 210mm Zeiss Tessar.

PAGES 22–23: Crowded geometric forms of the intensely urban Cliff Palace, seen across Cliff Canyon, Mesa Verde National Park, Colorado. 360mm Rodenstock.

PAGE 22 TOP LEFT: Basket Maker site at White Dog Cave, Arizona; re-created in a diorama in Mesa Verde Museum, Mesa Verde National Park, Colorado. 135mm Symmar. TOP RIGHT: Modified Basket Maker site in Step House Cave; diorama in Mesa Verde Museum. All, 135mm Symmar. BOTTOM: Developmental Pueblo village at harvest time; diorama in Mesa Verde Museum. 135mm Symmar.

PAGE 25: Classic Pueblo as evidenced at Spruce Tree House; diorama in Mesa Verde Museum. 135mm Symmar.

PAGES 26–27: Towers at Cliff Palace, Mesa Verde National Park, Colorado. 210mm Zeiss Tessar.

PAGE 27: Broad-leafed yucca. 210mm Zeiss Tessar.

PAGES 28–29: Cliff Palace in winter, Mesa Verde National Park, Colorado. 135mm Symmar.

PAGE 30: Dried corn and adobe. 210mm Zeiss Tessar.

PAGES 30–31: Village plaza and kiva entrance, Spruce Tree House, Mesa Verde National Park, Colorado. 75mm Super Angulon.

PAGE 32: Mug House interior, with kiva in foreground, Wetherill Mesa, Mesa Verde National Park, Colorado. 75mm Super Angulon.

PAGE 33: Rectangular window designs, Mug House, Mesa Verde National Park, Colorado. 100mm Wide-Field Ektar.

PAGE 34: T-design doorway, Mug House, Mesa Verde National Park, Colorado. 135mm Symmar.

PAGE 35: Long House, Wetherill Mesa, Mesa Verde National Park, Colorado. 100mm Wide-Field Ektar.

PAGE 36: Winter at Spruce Tree House, Mesa Verde National Park, Colorado. 135mm Symmar.

PAGE 37: Gentle spring greening at Long House, Wetherill Mesa, Mesa Verde National Park, Colorado. 210mm Zeiss Tessar.

PAGES 38–39: Unexcavated Spring House ruin, Long Mesa, Mesa Verde National Park, Colorado. 135mm Symmar.

PAGE 39: Mesa Verde–type canteen, Mesa Verde Museum, Mesa Verde National Park, Colorado. 210mm Zeiss Tessar.

PAGE 40: Sun Temple on Chapin Mesa, Mesa

Verde National Park, Colorado, with the Sierra La Plata in the background. 500mm Tele-Xenar.

PAGE 41. TOP: Detail in Balcony House, Mesa Verde National Park, Colorado. 135mm Symmar. BOTTOM: Symbolic petroglyph figures on sandstone patina above Navajo Canyon, Mesa Verde National Park, Colorado. 210mm Zeiss Tessar.

PAGE 42: Square Tower House, Mesa Verde National Park, Colorado. 210mm Zeiss Tessar.

PAGE 46: Three sandals from the Basket Maker Period, photographed in the Mesa Verde Museum, Mesa Verde National Park, Colorado. 135mm Symmar.

PAGE 49: Kayenta olla with schematic design photographed in Arizona State Museum, Tucson. 135mm Symmar.

PAGE 50: Autumn in Betatakin Canyon, Navajo National Monument, Arizona. 360mm Rodenstock.

PAGE 51: Quaking aspen at Betatakin, Navajo National Monument, Arizona. 210mm Zeiss Tessar.

PAGE 52: Window frame at Betatakin, Navajo National Monument, Arizona. 135mm Symmar.

PAGE 53: Re-creation of a cliff dwelling room, visitor center display, Navajo National Monument, Arizona. 100mm Wide-Field Ektar.

PAGES 54–55: Rhythm of natural and human forms in sandstone, Betatakin's west wall, Navajo National Monument, Arizona. 360mm Rodenstock.

PAGE 56. TOP: Kayenta-type olla, Arizona State Museum, Tucson. 135mm Symmar. BOTTOM: Arch and cliff dwelling at Keet Seel, Navajo National Monument, Arizona. 135mm Symmar.

PAGE 57: Kiva and other adobe structures, Keet Seel, Navajo National Monument, Arizona. 135-mm Symmar.

PAGES 58–59: Keet Seel interior, Navajo National Monument, Arizona. 100mm Wide-Field Ektar.

PAGE 60: Inscription House, in the upper reaches of Navajo Canyon wilderness, Navajo National Monument, Arizona. 75mm Super Angulon.

PAGE 61: Human and animal images in petroglyphs on sandstone patina, Tsegi Canyon, northern Arizona. 100mm Wide-Field Ektar.

PAGE 62: Potsherds in the snow, Longhouse Valley, northern Arizona. 210mm Zeiss Tessar.

PAGE 63: Ruin, Longhouse Valley, northern Arizona. 500mm Tele-Xenar.

PAGE 64: Petroglyphs, Puerco River, Petrified Forest National Park, Arizona. 100mm Wide-Field Ektar.

PAGE 67: Rain over Monument Valley, Arizona/Utah. 210mm Zeiss Tessar.

PAGE 73: Turquoise-decorated frogs: large frog from Kinisba; frog with feet, Hohokam; small frog, Sinagua, Verde Valley; photographed at Arizona State Museum, Tucson. 210mm Zeiss Tessar.

PAGES 74–75: Sunrise silhouette of Wukoki ruin, Wupatki National Monument, Arizona. 360mm Rodenstock.

PAGES 76–77: Tall House, Wupatki National Monument, Arizona. 360mm Rodenstock.

PAGES 78–79: Sunrise on the ruins at Lomaki, Wupatki National Monument, Arizona. 500mm Tele-Xenar.

PAGE 80: Sleeping volcano, Sunset Crater National Monument, Arizona. 135mm Symmar.

PAGE 81. LEFT: A Sinagua ruin, Walnut Canyon National Monument, Arizona. 210mm Zeiss Tessar. RIGHT: Walnut Canyon–type black-on-white pitcher and bowl, in Museum of Northern Arizona, Flagstaff. 210mm Zeiss Tessar.

PAGE 82: Grand Falls of the Little Colorado River, Arizona, at spring flood. 100mm Wide-Field Ektar.

PAGE 83: Grand Canyon of the Colorado from Mohave Point, Arizona. 500mm Tele-Xenar.

PAGE 84: Montezuma Well, Montezuma Castle National Monument, Arizona. 100mm Wide-Field Ektar.

PAGE 85: Cliff dwelling along Beaver Creek, Montezuma Castle National Monument, Arizona. 500-mm Tele-Xenar.

PAGE 86. TOP: Hilltop ruins of Tuzigoot National Monument, Arizona. Hasselblad 500C, 500mm Tele-Tessar. BOTTOM: Metate and mano with interior walls of ruin, Tuzigoot National Monument, Arizona. 210mm Zeiss Tessar.

PAGE 87: Gila polychrome pottery design from Roosevelt Basin; photographed in Arizona State Museum, Tucson. 135mm Symmar.

PAGES 88–89: Upper ruin, Tonto National Monument, Arizona. 135mm Symmar.

PAGE 89: Tonto polychrome vase from Roosevelt Basin; photographed in Arizona State Museum, Tucson. 135mm Symmar.

PAGES 90–91: Lower ruin with saguaro and cholla cacti, Tonto National Monument, Arizona. 360-mm Rodenstock.

PAGE 92: Cascade in the Santa Catalina Mountains, Arizona. 500mm Tele-Xenar.

PAGE 93. TOP: Hohokam ruin with recent protective canopy, Casa Grande National Monument, Arizona. 100mm Wide-Field Ektar. BOTTOM: Hohokam figure, Arizona State Museum, Tucson. 360-mm Rodenstock.

PAGE 94: Red-on-buff frog design (Hohokam Sedentary Period), Arizona State Museum, Tucson. 210mm Zeiss Tessar.

PAGE 95: Hohokam incense burner and bighorn sheep effigy (Sacaton Period), Arizona State Museum, Tucson. 210mm Zeiss Tessar.

PAGE 96: Mexican poppies, Tonto National Monument, Arizona. 500mm Tele-Xenar.

PAGE 103: Corrugated earthenware jars, Museum of Northern Arizona, Flagstaff. 210mm Zeiss Tessar.

PAGE 104: Monoliths at sunrise, Monument Valley Navajo Tribal Park, Arizona/Utah. 360mm Rodenstock.

PAGES 104–105: Sandstone ruin, Mystery Valley, Monument Valley Navajo Tribal Park, Arizona. 210mm Zeiss Tessar.

PAGE 106: Natural arch, Canyon de Chelly National Monument, Arizona. 135mm Symmar.

PAGE 107: White House ruin, Canyon de Chelly National Monument, Arizona. 500mm Tele-Xenar.

PAGE 108: Tower ruin, Horse Canyon, Canyonlands National Park, Utah. 500mm Tele-Xenar.

PAGE 110: Tower of Hovenweep National Monument, Utah/Colorado. 100mm Wide-Field Ektar.

PAGE 111. TOP: Gentle flow of springs with maidenhair fern, Kane Springs Canyon, Utah. 360mm Rodenstock. BOTTOM: "All-American Man" pictograph in Salt Creek Canyon, Canyonlands National Park, Utah. 210mm Zeiss Tessar.

PAGE 114: Square Tower ruins, Hovenweep National Monument, Utah. 135mm Symmar.

PAGE 117: Corrugated earthenware jar, Museum of Northern Arizona, Flagstaff. 135mm Symmar.

PAGE 118: Mesa Verde–type mug. Mesa Verde Museum, Mesa Verde National Park, Colorado. 135-mm Symmar.

PAGE 119. TOP: Petroglyphs in Little Rainbow Park, Dinosaur National Monument, Utah. 135mm Symmar. BOTTOM: Petroglyphs of men and buffalo in Little Rainbow Park, Dinosaur National Monument, Utah. 135mm Symmar.

PAGE 121: Mesa Verde–type black-on-white design found at Aztec National Monument, New Mexico. 135mm Symmar.

PAGE 122: Clan kiva and retaining walls, Pueblo Bonito, Chaco Canyon National Monument, New Mexico. 100mm Wide-Field Ektar.

PAGE 123: Interior walls, Chettro Kettle pueblo, Chaco Canyon National Monument, New Mexico. 100mm Wide-Field Ektar.

PAGE 124: Chaco-type black-on-white olla, photographed at the Museum of New Mexico, Santa Fe. 135mm Symmar.

PAGES 124–125: A great kiva at Pueblo Bonito, Chaco Canyon National Monument, New Mexico. 75mm Super Angulon.

PAGE 126: Eagle's view from canyon's north rim, showing D-shaped Pueblo Bonito, Chaco Canyon National Monument, New Mexico. 75mm Super Angulon.

PAGE 127: Rhythm of kiva circles seen from rim of Pueblo Bonito, Chaco Canyon National Monument, New Mexico. 500mm Tele-Xenar.

PAGE 128: Pueblo del Arroyo, Chaco Canyon National Monument, New Mexico. 135mm Symmar.

PAGE 129: Pueblo Alto, Chaco Canyon National Monument, New Mexico. 360mm Rodenstock.

PAGE 130: Great kiva interior, Casa Rinconada, Chaco Canyon National Monument, New Mexico. 75mm Super Angulon.

PAGE 131: Wall of stone and mortar, Chettro Kettle pueblo, Chaco Canyon National Monument, New Mexico. 210mm Zeiss Tessar.

PAGES 132–133: Kin Kletso ruin, Chaco Canyon National Monument, New Mexico. 100mm Wide-Field Ektar.

PAGES 134–135: Reconstructed interior of great kiva, Aztec National Monument, New Mexico. 75mm Super Angulon.

PAGE 135: Communal doorways, Aztec National Monument, New Mexico. 210mm Zeiss Tessar.

PAGE 136: Hatching design on Chaco-type pitcher, Aztec National Monument, New Mexico. 210mm Zeiss Tessar.

PAGE 140: Bird effigies from Tonto area, photographed in the Arizona State Museum, Tucson. 135mm Symmar.

PAGE 149: Flute player and shield petroglyph on volcanic rock, Galisteo Basin, New Mexico. 210-mm Zeiss Tessar.

PAGES 150–151: Kiva and mission church ruins at sunrise, Pecos National Monument, New Mexico. 100mm Wide-Field Ektar.

PAGE 152: Wild grasses and adobe ruins of mission church at Pecos National Monument, New Mexico. 135mm Symmar.

PAGE 153: Pueblo and Spanish missionary church ruins at Gran Quivira National Monument, New Mexico. 100mm Wide-Field Ektar.

PAGE 154: Kiva in Ceremonial Cave, Rito de los Frijoles Canyon, Bandelier National Monument, New Mexico. 75mm Super Angulon.

PAGE 155: Tyuonyi pueblo ruins, Rito de los Frijoles, Bandelier National Monument, New Mexico. 210mm Zeiss Tessar.

PAGE 156. TOP: Mimbres black-on-white bowl design, Museum of Northern Arizona, Flagstaff. 135mm Symmar. BOTTOM: Mother-and-child effigy, Casas Grandes pueblo ruins, Sonora, Mexico; photographed in the Arizona State Museum, Tucson. 135mm Symmar.

PAGE 157: Interior of ruins, Gila Cliff Dwellings National Monument, New Mexico. 100mm Wide-Field Ektar.

PAGE 158: Mimbres black-on-white bowl with human figures, Arizona State Museum, Tucson. 210mm Zeiss Tessar.

PAGE 159. TOP: Blooms of the narrow-leafed yucca. 500mm Tele-Xenar. BOTTOM: Lone cave with prickly pear cactus, Gila Cliff Dwellings National Monument, New Mexico. 75mm Super Angulon.

PAGE 160: Shield figure petroglyphs on volcanic rock, Galisteo Basin, New Mexico. 100mm Wide-Field Ektar.

PAGE 163: Zuñi owls, Denver Museum of Natural History. 135mm Symmar.

PAGE 167: Hopi Kachina figures, Laboratory of Anthropology, Museum of New Mexico, Santa Fe. 500mm Tele-Xenar.

PAGES 168–169: Spring corn planting at the Hopi village of Moenkopi, Arizona. 500mm Tele-Xenar.

PAGE 169: Full-grown Pueblo corn plant. 210mm Zeiss Tessar.

PAGES 170–171: Bread ovens and north plaza, Taos pueblo, New Mexico; Sangre de Cristo peaks in the background. 135mm Symmar.

PAGE 172: Modern Hopi polychrome design, Museum of Northern Arizona, Flagstaff. 135mm Symmar.

PAGE 173. TOP: Hano polychrome in modern winged design, Museum of Northern Arizona, Flagstaff. 135mm Symmar. BOTTOM: Santo Domingo pot, Museum of Northern Arizona, Flagstaff. 135mm Symmar.

PAGES 174–175: Ladders and old three-level dwelling at Ácoma, New Mexico. 201mm Zeiss Tessar.

PAGE 176: Distant view of Ácoma, New Mexico. Hasselblad 500C 500mm Tele-Tessar.

Acknowledgments

We greatly appreciate the generosity and cooperation of the many dedicated people in the national parks and monuments who made access to remote sites most rewarding for us, with a special thanks to Jim Court at Hovenweep National Monument and to Gil Wenger and the museum at Mesa Verde National Park. We are also most grateful to the curators and staffs of the following institutions for making their collections of pottery available for photography: the Arizona State Museum, University of Arizona, Tucson; Museum of Northern Arizona, Flagstaff; Maxwell Museum, University of New Mexico, Albuquerque; The Denver Museum of Natural History, Denver; and the Museum of New Mexico, Santa Fe.

We extend special appreciation to Robert A. Weinstein for his assistance in obtaining the Vroman photographs, and our thanks also to the Los Angeles County Museum for their cooperation in allowing us the use of portions of their Vroman collection.

Index

Body type: Trump Mediaeval, by Continental Graphics Typographers, Los Angeles. Display faces: Mosaik, by Paul O. Giesey/Adcrafters, Portland, Oregon; Delphin No. 2, by Atherton's Advertising Typography, Palo Alto, California. Separations and printing by Graphic Arts Center, Portland. *Design by Dannelle Lazarus and Bonnie Muench.*